A Guide to the Human l

A Guide to the
Human Rights Act 1998

Parosha Chandran, LLB, LLM,
Diploma in International and Comparative
Human Rights Law (Strasbourg)
Barrister

Butterworths
London, Edinburgh, Dublin
1999

United Kingdom	Butterworths a Division of Reed Elsevier (UK) Ltd, Halsbury House, 35 Chancery Lane, LONDON WC2A 1EL and 4 Hill Street, EDINBURGH EH2 3JZ
Australia	Butterworths, a Division of Reed International Books Australia Pty Ltd, CHATSWOOD, New South Wales
Canada	Butterworths Canada Ltd, MARKHAM, Ontario
Hong Kong	Butterworths Asia (Hong Kong), HONG KONG
India	Butterworths India, NEW DELHI
Ireland	Butterworth (Ireland) Ltd, DUBLIN
Malaysia	Malayan Law Journal Sdn Bhd, KUALA LUMPUR
New Zealand	Butterworths of New Zealand Ltd, WELLINGTON
Singapore	Butterworths Asia, SINGAPORE
South Africa	Butterworths Publishers (Pty) Ltd, DURBAN
USA	Lexis Law Publishing, CHARLOTTESVILLE, Virginia

A CIP Catalogue record for this book is available from the British Library.

ISBN 0 406 90520 7

Printed and bound in Great Britain by Redwood Books, Trowbridge, Wiltshire

Visit us at our website: http//www.butterworths.co.uk

For my parents
Raj and Qudsia Chandran

Preface

The purpose of this book is to provide a simple guide to the Human Rights Act 1998 by which certain of the rights protected by the European Convention on Human Rights 1950 are given further effect in UK law. Most notably the Act provides individuals with the right to challenge public authorities before the courts for having acted incompatibly with the Convention rights, and provides the courts with powers to grant effective remedies to individuals whose claims are upheld. Other features include a new system of pre-legislative scrutiny and a novel process by which primary legislation which does not comply with the Convention rights may be amended, in urgent cases by statutory instrument. The Act also makes provision in respect of UK judges appointed to the European Court of Human Rights in Strasbourg.

The Act bears great significance, not only in relation to individuals who were previously estopped from claiming violations to their Convention rights directly before the UK courts, but because of the introduction of a direction that all legislation must be read and given effect so far as possible in a manner that is compatible with the Convention rights. This direction will place the courts under the primary duty to uphold the protection of the Convention rights, and as a result when cases reach the Strasbourg Court, as some will inevitably do, the Court will have the benefit of considering a full and reasoned judgment on the interpretation of the Convention rights. It is hoped that this will reduce the number of violations found against the UK in Strasbourg.

The Human Rights Act 1998 places a heavy burden on the courts and legal practitioners to familiarise themselves with the Convention case law. The judiciary are currently undergoing training in this respect, and it is hoped that by the expected implementation date of 2 October 2000 the courts will be prepared to take on the tasks introduced by the 1998 Act. It is also essential for practitioners to prepare themselves thoroughly in understanding the Convention, its principles of interpretation and its jurisprudence.

This book provides an explanation of the provisions of the 1998 Act, comparing the significance of each new provision as far as practicable with the previous law. It must be noted however that any views expressed as to the meaning and effect of the new law are my own and are in many cases tentative. The Act is well-drafted, if brief, and its language is simple. This book is not intended to be a full exposition or analysis of the new law, but is instead intended as a guide to assist those who seek to make light of the significance of the Act's provisions. For this reason, extracts from the records of Hansard are included throughout.

I would like to express my warmest thanks to my family and friends who encouraged and supported me throughout the many months when I was "staying in with Hansard", and to those who offered inspiration, particularly Sir Nicolas Bratza QC, Marit Vik, Joy Elyahou and Ben Brandon. I would also like to thank my chambers, particularly Adam Clemens, for encouraging me to write this guide, Russell Jones and Walker solicitors for their generous support during the early stages of my research and my friends and colleagues at the International Criminal Tribunal for the Former Yugoslavia where I completed the first draft of this guide. In addition I offer my gratitude to the editorial staff at Butterworths for their hard work on this publication.

Parosha Chandran
Bridewell Chambers
November 1999

Contents

Table of Statutes

European Convention
(Table of Articles and Protocols)

1 Introduction

OVERVIEW OF HRA 1998

1.1   The Human Rights Act 1998 (HRA 1998), received Royal Assent on 9 November 1998 and is intended to give 'further effect' to certain rights and freedoms protected by the European Convention on Human Rights 1950 (the Convention) (see Ch 2). Although the main provisions of HRA 1998 are expected to come into force on 2 October 2000, courts and tribunals in the UK are already hearing cases raising human rights issues in anticipation of the Act's commencement.

1.2   The 1998 Act is a tightly-drafted piece of legislation, containing only 22 sections, each of considerable significance. Its enactment will have a major impact on individuals, courts, public authorities and the legal profession. Its effects will permeate all sections of society and will undoubtedly lead to a culture of human rights awareness in the UK.

1.3   First, HRA 1998 makes accessible the rights and freedoms termed 'the Convention rights' for the purposes of the 1998 Act to all persons directly or potentially affected by actions of public authorities who act or propose to act incompatibly with, ie in breach of, the Convention right(s). It permits such persons to apply to the domestic courts to enforce their Convention rights and, where a breach is upheld, to be granted remedies against the public authority. Secondly, and crucially, it requires public authorities to act compatibly with the Convention rights, making it unlawful to act in a contrary manner. Thirdly, it introduces a new method of interpretation, by which all legislation must be read and given effect so far as possible in a manner that is compatible with the Convention rights. This new obligation will apply not only to courts and tribunals, but to any person or organisation authorised to read and give effect to legislation. Fourthly, HRA 1998 requires all courts and tribunals to take into account relevant Strasbourg case law whenever a question concerning a Convention right is raised in the proceedings. Fifthly, a new and fast mechanism for amending incompatible legislation in cases where to amend by primary legislation would be inefficient is created. Finally, the 1998 Act provides for a public method of pre-legislative scrutiny by way of a ministerial statement, to be placed before each House of Parliament before the Second Reading of a Government Bill.

1.4   The various provisions of HRA 1998 work effectively together to produce a legal charter which provides efficient measures for promoting respect for the rights and fundamental freedoms of the Convention. Unfortunately these provisions fall short of creating a Human Rights Commission to provide independent education, consultation and advice on human rights issues to both individuals and public authorities. Also the provisions of HRA 1998 do not provide a water-tight protection against future incompatible legislation being passed by Parliament. Nonetheless, the 1998 Act contains valuable mechanisms to protect Convention rights from infringement and to provide redress for breaches. As such it will be acceptable to many of those who claim that rights guaranteed under the Convention have been ignored for too long by the Executive, the legislature and the judiciary in the UK.

1.5   Certain features of HRA 1998 are discussed below, as follows—
     — Protecting the Convention rights
     — The scope of the interpretative obligation
     — Judicial aids to interpretation
     — Public authorities
     — Bringing proceedings for breach and the 'victim test'
     — Remedies for breach and 'just satisfaction'.

PROTECTING THE CONVENTION RIGHTS

1.6   HRA 1998, s 1 defines the Convention rights as being those contained in Arts 2–12 and 14 of the Convention, Arts 1–3 of the First Protocol and Arts 1 and 2 of the Sixth Protocol. Specifically these comprise—
     — the right to life (Art 2),
     — the prohibition of torture (Art 3),
     — the prohibition of slavery and forced labour (Art 4),
     — the right to liberty and security (Art 5),
     — the right to a fair trial (Art 6),
     — no punishment without law (Art 7),
     — the right to respect for private and family life (Art 8),
     — freedom of thought, conscience and religion (Art 9),
     — freedom of expression (Art 10),
     — freedom of assembly and association (Art 11),
     — the right to marry (Art 12),
     — the prohibition of discrimination (Art 14),
     — the protection of property (First Protocol, Art 1),
     — the right to education (First Protocol, Art 2),
     — the right to free elections (First Protocol, Art 3), and
     — freedom from the death penalty in peace time (Sixth Protocol).

Each of these rights is to be 'read with' Art 16 (restrictions on political activity of aliens), Art 17 (prohibition of abuse of rights) and Art 18 (limitation on use of restrictions on rights).

1.7   Under HRA 1998 it will be unlawful for public authorities to act incompatibly with the Convention rights (s 6), the Convention rights may form the basis of actions or may be relied upon in any legal proceedings (s 7) and remedies, including damages, may be claimed for breach by a public authority (ss 8, 9). The Convention rights are thus strongly incorporated into HRA 1998, a fact which will go some way in promoting the respect for and the protection of those rights.

1.8   It is important to note that the nature and scope of certain of the Convention rights differ. For example, the right to freedom from torture, inhuman and degrading treatment or punishment (Art 3) is an absolute right and may not be interfered with by the State under any conditions. In contrast to this the rights protected by Arts 8–11 (private and family life, religion, expression and association) may be legitimately interfered with by the State where the State can prove, for example, that it was acting in accordance with the law or that the interference was necessary in a democratic society. In such cases the State must also prove that any interference was proportionate to the legitimate aim being pursued. Further, the right to freedom from discrimination protected by Art 14 is the only Convention right which is not free-standing, and under the Convention scheme a complaint to the European Court of Human Rights (the Strasbourg Court) regarding Art 14 must be accompanied by a complaint concerning another Convention right, albeit that the court may find a breach of Art 14 alone. Arguably, the same joinder of Art 14 claims will be required when a Convention rights complaint is made to the domestic courts.

1.9   Recourse must be had to the Convention case law in determining the nature and scope of each of the Convention rights and the conditions under which a State may argue legitimate interference, together with the extent of the interference permitted. For the purposes of HRA 1998, the public authorities take on the role of the State in protecting the Convention rights from abuse: the Convention case law is the jurisprudence of HRA 1998 and public authorities must abide by its principles.

1.10   Article 1 (the basic obligation upon States to secure to everyone within their jurisdiction the rights and freedoms guaranteed in the Convention) and Art 13 (the right to an effective remedy) are omitted from the list of the Convention rights contained in HRA 1998, s 1, as the Government considers that they are given effect by the passing of the 1998 Act (see para 3.14).[1]

---

[1]   See also paras 10.12–10.14.

1.11   While the omission of Art 1 poses no serious problems, the exclusion of Art 13 will mean that Parliament may pass legislation in the future that is incompatible with the Convention. This prospect is anticipated by HRA 1998, s 19, which requires a minister to provide a statement at Second Reading of a Bill in each House of Parliament attesting either that a Bill is compatible with the Convention rights or that whilst he cannot state that it is compatible the Government nonetheless wishes the Bill to proceed (see further Ch 18). Of course, should Parliament enact incompatible legislation after HRA 1998 comes into force, the right to apply to the European Court of Human Rights in Strasbourg for redress will remain available for any person affected potentially or directly by such legislation.

THE SCOPE OF THE INTERPRETATIVE OBLIGATION

1.12   After HRA 1998 comes into force all legislation must be read so far as possible in a way that is compatible with the Convention rights (s 3) (see further Ch 5). The wording of s 3 demonstrates the limited extent to which Parliament has incorporated the Convention into domestic law. The 1998 Act expressly limits the interpretative obligation, and does not extend it to promoting the Convention rights over existing or future legislation, ie the implied repeal of such legislation will not apply in respect of HRA 1998. However HRA 1998 has a special constitutional significance: no subsequent legislation can implicitly repeal the Act's provisions.

1.13   The obligation to read legislation together with the Convention rights under s 3 is directed only 'so far as it is possible' (s 3(1)). Where primary legislation or subordinate legislation made thereunder makes a compatible interpretation impossible, by reason that the legislation irreconcilably conflicts with the Convention rights, s 3 directs that such incompatible legislation will remain in force and will continue to have validity and effect. Where legislation is found to be incompatible, a higher court may make a declaration of incompatibility (s 4), the Crown first having been given notice of the intended declaration and having had the right to intervene before such declaration is made (s 5). A declaration under s 4 will not affect the continuing validity, enforcement or operation of the incompatible legislation, and furthermore is not binding on the parties (s 4(6)).

1.14 The power to overrule or strike down incompatible legislation has not been given to the courts. Instead Parliament has the option to amend such legislation by way of remedial action (s 10) and remedial orders (Sch 2) (see further Ch 12). Any risk of parliamentary sovereignty being undermined is thus abrogated, as the court's role in dealing with incompatible primary legislation is limited to providing a formal indication of that incompatibility by way of a s 4 declaration.

1.15 By limiting the interpretative obligation under HRA 1998, s 3, the Convention rights do not, unlike Directives passed pursuant to European Community law, have direct effect, ie automatic primacy before UK courts over domestic legislation. Instead, for the Convention rights to be enforced through the courts it is necessary for legislation to first be found to be compatible with the Convention rights. Only then can an assessment be made by the courts as to whether and to what extent the rights have been breached, and as to the nature of the remedies that may follow. On the other hand, where the legislation is found to be incompatible with the Convention rights, all a higher court may do is issue a declaration of incompatibility. In such cases an individual will have to claim remedies from the Strasbourg Court if he so wishes, since the offending legislation will remain in force in the UK unless and until amended by ordinary Parliamentary procedure or by remedial orders under HRA 1998 (see para 6.17).

1.16 It should be noted that the interpretative obligation under s 3 is not applicable only to courts and tribunals, but extends to any person or organisation authorised to read and give effect to legislation.

1.17 It will also be necessary for the common law to give effect to the Convention rights, in line with Parliament's intentions in enacting HRA 1998. However, whereas courts interpreting statute law will be able to do so only in respect of the Convention rights as defined in HRA 1998, s 1, judges acting under the common law may not be so restrained. For example, judges may find that they can develop the common law with Art 13 in mind, particularly in relation to the grant of remedies for breach (see paras 10.15–10.19).

JUDICIAL AIDS TO INTERPRETATION

1.18 By virtue of HRA 1998, s 2 a court or tribunal must take into account determinations of certain Strasbourg institutions when determining a question which has arisen in connection with a Convention right (see further Ch 4). As is apparent from the phraseology of the Articles comprising the Convention rights, those who drafted the Convention after the Second World War chose to set out the rights and fundamental freedoms protected by the Convention in a simple unobstructed manner, no doubt anticipating that the case-law of the Strasbourg institutions would define and detail the content of those Articles on a case by case basis. The jurisprudence of the Convention is now extremely sophisticated, and each of the Convention rights has a large volume of determinations emanating from the Commission, the Committee of Ministers and the Court which refine considerably the purpose, meaning and scope of each Article.

1.19 For the Convention rights to be effectively protected, it is essential for the courts to comply with the direction contained within s 2. Not only is regard to Strasbourg case law vital in interpreting the nature of each of the Convention rights and to what extent interference by the State is permissible, but in practice should a court fail to consider relevant Strasbourg decisions when determining questions which have arisen in connection with a Convention right, it might later find itself subject to proceedings for acting unlawfully, ie in a manner that was not compatible with a Convention right (see para 1.20).

THE CONDUCT OF PUBLIC AUTHORITIES

1.20 It is unlawful for a public authority to act in a manner that is incompatible with the Convention rights (s 6(1)). Only where a public authority was prevented by primary legislation from acting differently or where a public authority was acting to enforce incompatible primary legislation does the prohibition not apply (s 6(2)) (see further Ch 8).

1.21 The reason for the focus on public authorities is that the UK is liable before the Strasbourg court for the actions of public authorities acting in breach of the Convention provisions. The s 6 prohibition is therefore intended to force public authorities to bring their practices into line with the Convention rights, resulting in fewer breaches of the Convention committed by public authorities than in the past and a reduction in the number of cases which come before the Strasbourg Court.

BRINGING PROCEEDINGS FOR BREACH

1.22 Those who claim that their Convention rights have been infringed, or are about to be infringed, by a public authority failing to act compatibility with one or more Convention rights, may bring proceedings under HRA 1998 for that breach (s 7) (see further Ch 9). Two forms of action are provided by HRA 1998. First, free-standing actions may be brought against a public authority directly to enforce one or more of the Convention rights (s 7(1)(a)). A limitation period of one year from the date of the act complained of applies to free-standing actions under s 7, although the courts may extend the time where it is equitable in the circumstances to do so (s 7(5)). However, this is subject to any stricter limitation period which applies, for example three months where Convention rights are to be raised in judicial review proceedings (see para 9.7).

1.23 Secondly, the Convention rights may be relied upon in any legal proceedings to which a public authority is party, for example actions brought by a public authority or appeals against the decision of a court or tribunal (s 7(1)(b)). A complainant may therefore raise an argument concerning the Convention right(s) as a defence to a criminal action, as a counterclaim to civil proceedings or as a ground of judicial review. It is expected that the majority of actions will be brought using this method.

THE 'VICTIM TEST'

1.24 The test of standing for bringing proceedings under either of these methods is the 'victim test', a new concept imported into domestic law from Strasbourg, The victim test requires that for a person to bring proceedings to uphold the Convention rights the person must be directly or potentially affected by the act complained about. The test adopted by HRA 1998 is the same as the test of standing for actions brought by applicants before the Strasbourg Court (s 7(7)), which has found inter alia, adults, children, private companies, spouses and parents of the deceased persons to be victims.

1.25 The victim test is to apply strictly in the domestic courts under HRA 1998, even where the proceedings concerned are judicial review proceedings. This has the undesirable effect of creating two separate tests of standing in judicial review proceedings, dependent upon whether Convention rights are raised as grounds for judicial review or not. Where Convention rights are raised, the victim test of standing must be satisfied, whereas in judicial review cases not involving Convention rights the test remains that of proving sufficient interest.

1.26 Paradoxically, therefore, whereas representative groups and non-governmental organisations have been able to show 'sufficient interest' in the past to bring judicial review proceedings in cases raising issues of public importance and fundamental rights, under HRA 1998 such groups will not pass the victim test unless they are directly or potentially affected. They will therefore not be able to bring judicial review proceedings in their own name where Convention rights are raised as grounds for the application. There is nothing of course in the 1998 Act which prohibits such groups from supporting litigants, and it seems likely that the courts will admit amicus briefs from such organisations during the course of proceedings.

REMEDIES FOR BREACH AND 'JUST SATISFACTION'

1.27 Where a court upholds a complaint that a public authority has acted or proposes to act in breach of one or more of the Convention rights it may award any remedy which it has the power to grant under its existing powers (s 8) (see further Ch 10). The court may extend by order the remedies a tribunal may grant by virtue of s 7(11), although this is aimed particularly at broadening the remedial powers of Special Adjudicators in immigration tribunals (see para 9.23). In the main, however, courts will be restricted by their existing statutory or common law powers to grant remedies. Furthermore HRA 1998 specifically provides that a court which does not have pre-existing powers to award damages or to grant compensation in civil proceedings may not grant damages to a successful complainant (s 8(2)). Instead, the successful party will have to pursue compensation through the civil courts.

1.28 In determining whether to award damages or the amount of an award, the domestic courts are directed to take into account the principles applied by the Strasbourg Court in awarding compensation to a successful complainant (s 8(4)). This means taking into account the Strasbourg case law on the interpretation of 'just satisfaction' under Art 41 of the Convention, the provision by which the Strasbourg Court is empowered to award damages (see paras 10.6–10.8).

1.29 In many human rights cases the Strasbourg Court cannot restore the successful complainant of a Convention breach to the *status quo ante*, and in such cases financial compensation is the only realistic consideration for the Court. The Court generally applies its power to award damages restrictively, and in some the cases will award no financial compensation at all by reason that the finding of a violation was a sufficient remedy in itself. Whenever damages are awarded as just satisfaction, the sum awarded will have to be determined by the Court on an equitable basis.

1.30 Where the Court has found a causal link between the damage suffered and the breach of the Convention, the Court will consider awarding damages for pecuniary loss (quantifiable loss such as loss of income). The Court's case law indicates that its calculation of any award depends upon the facts of each particular case, taking into account all the relevant circumstances and the extent of the damage caused. When awarding damages for non-pecuniary loss, (ie pain and suffering, and mental or physical injury), the Court does not quantify its award nor give anything more than brief reasoning in doing so. When awarding both pecuniary and non-pecuniary damages, the Court does not specify the proportion of each. Whereas the Court has regularly awarded damages of a pecuniary and non-pecuniary nature, it has not awarded punitive or exemplary damages to date. Such an award is not ruled out however in an appropriate case in the future. As to costs and expenses, the Court usually awards these, although it will not award the entire sum of costs if it finds the sum to be excessive.

1.31 Generally speaking, the Court's awards for human rights breaches are modest in comparison to damages awarded by the domestic courts for breach of tortious or contractual rights. Consequently, by requiring the domestic courts to take into account the Strasbourg Court's assessment of 'just satisfaction', HRA 1998 does not intend to provide a vehicle for large awards of damages where an unlawful act by a public authority is found to have taken place. Further and notably, damages cannot be awarded by the courts under HRA 1998 for an unlawful judicial act done in good faith, except in one strict case, namely to compensate a person who was unlawfully detained in contravention of Art 5(5) of the Convention (s 9) (see Ch 11).

CONCLUSIONS

1.32 The Act will arguably prove a strong form of incorporation of the Convention rights, and its early implementation is desirable. The obligation upon public authorities to bring their practices in line with the Convention rights and the onus upon the courts in particular to seek to protect those rights from infringement by reading and giving effect to legislation in compliance with the Convention rights so far as possible will undoubtedly lead to a culture of human rights awareness developing in the UK. On the international front, where cases alleging Convention breaches which emanate from the

UK arrive for consideration by the Strasbourg Court, the Court will be able to operate as an *ex post facto* system of review as originally intended by the Convention draftsmen and not as the primary decision-maker, a role it was forced to take on in relation to UK cases where Convention breaches were alleged. Insofar as the admissibility of applications to the Court are concerned, the applicant will in most cases have to show that he first raised his Convention rights before the domestic courts, as he can now do under HRA 1998, s 7, in order to satisfy the 'exhaustion of domestic remedies' rule of the Convention.

1.33 The enactment of HRA 1998 is a positive step forward for the UK in supporting the rights of the individual against unlawful State interference and in securing compliance with and respect for the rule of law. It will bring UK law into line with the internationally recognised expectation that human rights will be respected and that a State will refrain from violating those rights of persons within its jurisdiction and will act positively to protect such rights where required to do so.

2 The purpose of the Human Rights Act 1998

INTENTION BEHIND THE LEGISLATION

2.1   The long title of the Human Rights Act 1998 (HRA 1998) is 'An Act to give further effect to rights and freedoms guaranteed under the European Convention on Human Rights; to make provision with respect to holders of certain judicial offices who become judges of the European Court of Human Rights; and for connected purposes'.

2.2   In respect of the first part of the long title it is noticeable that the 1998 Act does not purport to give 'direct' effect to Convention rights and freedoms, but instead provides for 'further effect' to be given to them. At the Report stage in the House of Lords, the Lord Chancellor, Lord Irvine of Lairg, explained what this meant—

> 'The word 'further' is included in the Long Title because, in our national arrangements, the Convention can, and is, already applied in a variety of different circumstances and is relied on in a range of ways by our own courts.'[1]

---

[1]   HL Report, 29 January 1998, col 421.

PREVIOUS APPLICATION OF CONVENTION

2.3   Prior to the enactment of HRA 1998, it was possible for the courts to apply the Convention in various ways. Five examples of situations in which the courts can already take the Convention into account were given during the early debates on the Bill,[1] as follows—

— where a statute is capable of two interpretations, one consistent with the Convention and the other inconsistent, the courts will presume that Parliament intended to legislate in conformity with the Convention;

— where the common law is uncertain, unclear or incomplete, the courts will rule wherever possible in a manner that complies with the Convention;

— where a domestic statute is enacted to fulfil a Convention obligation the courts will ordinarily assume that the statute was intended to effect the Convention obligation;

— where the courts must decide what, in a given situation, public policy demands, they have regard to the UK's international obligations, including those under the Convention, as a source of guidance;

— where the proceedings concern directly effective EU law, the courts will take the Convention into account because EU law enshrines human rights principles, including those guaranteed by the Convention.[2]

After citing these examples Lord Irvine commented, 'Every lawyer knows this. No one can conceivably think that we intend to enact anything other than an Act to give further effect within the United Kingdom to a Convention which already has effect in our domestic law.'

---
[1]   HL Committee, 18 November 1997, col 478, drawing upon the earlier comments of Lord Bingham of Cornhill at HL Debates, 3 July 1996, col 1465.
[2]   HL Committee, 18 November 1997, col 479.

2.4   In explaining why the Convention rights cannot be said to be fully 'incorporated' into UK law, Lord Irvine said—

> 'The Bill will greatly increase the ability of our courts to enforce Convention rights, but it is not introducing a wholly new concept . . . the Bill as such does not incorporate Convention rights into domestic law but, in accordance with the language of the Long Title, it gives further effect in the United Kingdom to Convention rights by requiring the courts in Clause 3(1),
>
> > 'so far as it is possible to do',
>
> to construe—in the language of the statute, to read and give effect to—primary legislation and subordinate legislation in a way which is compatible with the Convention rights. That is an interpretative principle. . . .
>
> I have to make this point absolutely plain. The European Convention on Human Rights under this Bill is not made part of our law.
>
> . . .
>
> The short point is that if the Convention rights were incorporated into our law, they would be *directly justiciable* and would be enforced by our courts. That is not the scheme of this Bill. If the courts find it impossible to construe primary legislation in a way which is compatible with the Convention rights, the primary legislation remains in full force and effect. All that the courts may do is to make a declaration of incompatibility'[author's emphasis].[1]

---
[1]   HL Report, 29 January 1998, cols 421–422.

VERTICAL OR HORIZONTAL EFFECT?

2.5   Lord Irvine explained the scope of protection offered by HRA 1998 to private individuals as follows—

> 'What the Bill does not do is to make the Convention rights themselves directly a part of our domestic law in the same way that, for example, the civil wrongs of negligence, trespass or libel are part of our domestic law. Claims in those areas are all actionable in tort in cases between private individuals. . . . We have sought to protect the human rights of individuals against the abuse of power by the State, broadly defined, rather than to protect them against each other. That is the only practical difference between the full incorporation of the Convention rights into our domestic law and the actual effect of the Bill.'[1]

---
[1]   HL 3R, 5 February 1998, col 840.

2.6   The purpose of the 1998 Act, as perceived by Lord Irvine, is to regulate the dealings of the State with private individuals (the vertical effect), not the dealings vis-à-vis individuals (the horizontal effect). It may be recalled that only the actions of public authorities are made unlawful under s 6 for non-compliance with the Convention rights. Actions by private individuals are outside the scope of that section. However, a duty is imposed upon courts and tribunals under s 2 to take into account Strasbourg case law whenever a Convention question is raised which is relevant to the proceedings, and further, under s 3 the courts must read domestic legislation and give effect to it in a way which is compatible with the Convention rights if it is possible to do so. Consequently, in practical terms there is a real prospect of the Convention rights being taken into account in *all* proceedings before the court, not just those proceedings where a public authority is a party. Furthermore, this approach would not be inconsistent with the case law of the Convention which shows that for certain of the rights to be effectively protected, it may be necessary for the domestic courts to regulate the conduct between private individuals with Convention rights in mind. This is particularly so in relation to the rights protected by Art 2 (the right to life), Art 3 (prohibition of torture) and Art 8 (the right to respect for private and family life, home and correspondence), where the Convention case law requires a State to take positive steps to protect such rights, and not merely to abstain from violating them.

3 The Convention rights

DEFINITION OF CONVENTION RIGHTS

3.1   During the Second Reading of the Human Rights Bill, the Lord Chancellor, Lord Irvine of Lairg, stated—

> '[Section] 1 lists the Convention rights that are to be given further effect in the United Kingdom by the [Act]. They range from the right to a fair trial to the right to life itself; and they are all fundamental human rights. The text is set out in Schedule 1 to the [Act]. Also, [section] 1 makes it possible for the rights contained in other protocols to be added to the [Act] if the United Kingdom becomes a party to them in the future.'[1]

---

[1]   HL 2R, 3 November 1997, col 1230.

3.2   The Human Rights Act 1998 (HRA 1998), s 1(1) defines the Convention rights as being those set out in certain Articles of the Convention and the First and Sixth Protocols (see para 1.6), and these are reproduced in Sch 1. The Convention rights include all substantive rights guaranteed under the Convention which have been ratified by the UK with the exception of Art 13. Also excluded from the 1998 Act are the preamble to and Art 1 of the Convention.

3.3   The Convention rights are to be 'read with' Arts 16 to 18 of the Convention, also set out in Sch 1 to the Act (s 1(1)). Article 16 states that nothing in Arts 10 (freedom of expression), 11 (freedom of assembly and association) and 14 (prohibition of discrimination) of the Convention 'shall be regarded as preventing the High Contracting Parties from imposing restrictions on the political activity of aliens.'. Article 17 of the Convention aims to protect substantive Convention rights from destruction or limitation by States or individuals beyond that authorised by the Convention. Article 18 prohibits a State from permitting restrictions on Convention rights for purposes other than those which the rights themselves prescribe.

Derogation and reservation

3.4   The Convention rights are 'to have effect for the purposes of this Act' (s 1(2)). This is subject to any designated derogation or reservation entered into by the UK. HRA 1998, ss 14–17 define such limitations and the domestic procedure which is to be followed concerning such matters (see further Ch 16). To date, the UK has entered into one derogation (concerning the lawful periods of detention for those suspected of terrorist activities relating to Northern Ireland) and one reservation (concerning the right to the provision of education). Schedule 3 sets out the terms of the UK's derogation from Art 15(3) of the Convention (Sch 3, Pt I) and reservation to Art 2 to the First Protocol to the Convention (Sch 3, Pt II).

Adding Protocols to the Convention rights

3.5   Provision is made in HRA 1998, s 1 for the likelihood that the UK may become a party to other Protocols of the Convention in the future. Under s 1(4) the 1998 Act can be amended by order of the Secretary of State, in a way he considers appropriate to 'reflect the effect' of a protocol. Section 1(5) defines a 'Protocol' as a Protocol to the Convention which the UK has ratified or has signed with view to ratification. Section 1(6) provides that an order under s 1(4) may only be made after the Protocol is in force in the UK. Thus far, no other Protocols have been added to the list of Convention rights, although it is likely that Protocol 7 will be ratified by the UK and after it has entered into force will then be added to HRA 1998 by the Secretary of State. This will occur once Parliament has legislated to amend some provisions of family law that are incompatible with the rights protected by Protocol 7 (see further para 19.4).

THE SIXTH PROTOCOL AND THE ABOLITION OF THE DEATH PENALTY

3.6   The inclusion of Arts 1 and 2 of the Sixth Protocol in HRA 98 came at a late stage of the Bill's progress through Parliament, bringing about the abolition of the death penalty in the UK. This occurred as a result of free vote in the House of Commons, during the Committee stage of the Bill.[1] The Commons overwhelmingly voted, by 294 votes to 136, to extend the incorporation of the Convention so as to include the as yet unratified sixth protocol (abolition of the death penalty in peacetime).

---

[1]   HC Committee, 20 May 1998, cols 987–1012.

3.7   Kevin McNamara, in proposing the amendment, explained to the House of Commons—

'. . . as a House, we abolished the death penalty for a trial period in 1965. That was made permanent in 1969 for this island and in 1973 for Northern Ireland.

There remained on the statute book two crimes which carried the death penalty: treason and piracy. However, as a result of an amendment, tabled in another place . . . to [section 36] of the Crime and Disorder [Act 1998], those crimes were removed from the statute book.'[1]

---

[1]   HC Committee, 20 May 1998, col 987.

3.8   Following the free vote to incorporate the Sixth Protocol provisions into the 1998 Act, all that remained for the death penalty to be finally abolished was to amend the relevant domestic law on military offences, namely the provisions of the Army Act 1955, the Air Force Act 1955 and the Naval Discipline Act 1957. These amendments were introduced by the Home Secretary, Jack Straw, in the House of Commons on 21 October 1998, whereupon the Government's intention to ratify the Sixth Protocol was clarified by Mike O'Brien, Parliamentary Under-Secretary of State for the Home Department, as follows—

'. . . amendment No 31 inserts a new subsection into [section] 21, which provides that any liability to the death penalty under the Armed Forces Acts is to be treated as a liability to life imprisonment or some lesser penalty instead.

. . . Amendment No 32 provides that the new subsection inserted by amendment No 31 comes into force when the Bill receives Royal Assent.

That is consistent with our intention to honour the decision of the House by proceeding without delay to sign and ratify the sixth protocol.

. . . Amendment No 34 provides that the new subsection inserted by amendment No 31 has effect in any place in which the Armed Forces Acts have effect, which is necessary because, unlike the Human Rights Bill, those acts are not limited in their territorial extent to the United Kingdom'.[1]

---

[1]   HC Report, 21 October 1998, col 1353.

3.9   As to the ramifications of the amendments, Mike O'Brien continued—

' . . . The practical effects of the amendments are such that Parliament will not be able to reintroduce the death penalty, other than for acts committed in time of war or imminent threat of war, unless the United Kingdom denounces the European Convention on human rights.'[1]

---

[1]   HC Report, 21 October 1998, col 1354.

3.10 The amendments are incorporated into HRA 1998, s 21(5), which states—

'Any liability under the Army Act 1955, the Air Force Act 1955 or the Naval Discipline Act 1957 to suffer death for an offence is replaced by a liability to imprisonment for life or any less punishment authorised by those Acts; and those Acts shall accordingly have effect with the necessary modifications.'

Section 21(5) extends to any place to which the Armed Forces Acts apply, ie to acts by military personnel at home and abroad (s 22(7)).

3.11 The permitted use of the death penalty in time of war is contained in Art 2 of the Sixth Protocol, which provides—

'A State may make provision in its law for the death penalty in respect of acts committed in time of war or of imminent threat of war; such penalty shall be applied only in the instances laid down in the law and in accordance with its provisions. The State shall communicate to the Secretary General of the Council of Europe the relevant provisions of that law.'[1]

---

[1]   See also HRA 1998, Sch 1, para 1.

3.12 Upon consideration of the Commons' Amendments by the House of Lords, Lord Lester explained the importance of the UK's acceptance to ratify the Sixth Protocol—

'The protocol has been ratified by all the European Union States with the exception of the United Kingdom. It has also been ratified by 28 of the 40 Council of Europe States. So far as I am aware, the death penalty has been abolished from Ireland in the west to Turkey in the east in 40 member States . . . it seems to me that no one can say that what we are doing has not been carefully considered by both Houses or is out of line with general standards across the European system which includes a variety of legal and cultural traditions . . . we are [also] very glad to hear that the position in the Channel Islands is to be brought into line . . .'[1]

---

[1]   HL Consideration of Commons Amendments, 29 October 1998, col 2087.

THE EXCLUSION OF ARTS 1 AND 13 OF THE CONVENTION

3.13 There was considerable debate during the Bill's passage through Parliament regarding the omission of Art 13 and, to a lesser extent, the omission of Art 1. Article 1 of the Convention provides that the High Contracting Parties shall secure to everyone within their jurisdiction the rights and freedoms set out in the Convention, Arts 2–18. Under Art 13 of the Convention, 'Everyone whose rights and freedoms as set forth in this Convention are violated shall have an effective remedy before a national authority'.

3.14 During the Second Reading in the House of Lords Lord Irvine explained why Arts 1 and 13 had been excluded from the list of Convention rights enumerated within HRA 1998, s 1—

'The Bill gives effect to Article 1 by securing to the people in the United Kingdom the rights and freedoms of the Convention. It gives effect to Article 13 by establishing a scheme under which Convention rights can be raised before our domestic courts. To that end, remedies are provided in [section] 8.'[1]

---

[1]   HL Committee, 18 November 1997, col 475.

3.15 Lord Williams of Mostyn, Under-Secretary of State at the Home Office, was more direct when he stated that 'Our view is, quite unambiguously, that Article 13 is met by the passage of the Bill.'[1]

---

[1]   HL 2R, 3 November 1998, col 1308.

3.16 The central purpose of the 1998 Act may be taken as guaranteeing individuals in the UK the protection of their Convention rights, and ensuring an effective remedy before the national courts where those rights are breached.

3.17 References to the omission of Art 13 continued during the passage of the Bill through Parliament, and attempts were made by Opposition members to include it. At Committee Stage in the House of Commons Jack Straw, speaking against such an amendment proposed by Sir Nicholas Lyle, gave a more revealing explanation as to why it had been omitted—

'. . . it is the Bill that gives effect to Article 13, so there was an issue of duplication . . . In considering Article 13, the courts could decide to grant damages in more circumstances than we had envisaged. We had to consider that matter carefully, because of the effect on the public purse. We are dealing with breaches of rights by public bodies, some of which are financed by Government—whose purse is, apparently, endless and seamless—whereas others do not have access to the full resources of Her Majesty's Government and the Bank of England printing works in my home town of Loughton in Essex. We had to think carefully about the scope of the remedies that we should provide.

Our overall judgment is that the amendment, which would incorporate Article 13, would not add anything much, but might create uncertainties. We see no particular reason to accept it.'[1]

---

[1]   HC Committee, 20 May 1998, col 979.

3.18 As explained by Jack Straw the omission of Art 13 is tied directly to the intended scope and extent of remedies which a court may grant under HRA 1998 (see paras 10.12–10.14). However, the courts may have regard to Art 13 where relevant to the proceedings (see paras 4.19–4.21).

4 The interpretation of Convention rights

STRASBOURG DETERMINATIONS

4.1 Section 2(1) states that 'A court or tribunal determining a question which has arisen in connection with a Convention right *must take into account*' various determinations of the Strasbourg Court, the Commission and the Committee of Ministers 'whenever made or given, so far as, in the opinion of the court or tribunal, it is *relevant* to the proceedings in which that question has arisen.' [author's emphasis].

4.2 The Strasbourg determinations which the domestic court or tribunal[1] must take into account include judgments, decisions, declarations and advisory opinions of the Court, opinions taken on the merits of a case by the Commission, decisions on admissibility taken by the Commission and decisions of the merits of a case taken by the Committee of Ministers.[2] All such determinations, whether made before or after the enactment of the Human Rights Act 1998 (HRA 1998), are included.

---

[1]   Section 21 defines 'tribunal' as 'any tribunal in which legal proceedings may be brought'.
[2]   Section 2(1)(a)–(d); see further para 19.9.

Committee of Ministers

4.3 It should be noted that the role of the Committee of Ministers, a politically-appointed body, in the consideration of violations alleged under the Convention, has been abolished by Protocol 11 to the Convention which entered into force on 1 November 1998. The Committee of Ministers, however, continues its role in supervising the execution of final judgments of the Court under Art 46(2) of the Convention and in requesting advisory opinions of the Court under Art 47. Protocol 11 also replaced the two-tier Commission and Court structure by a single Court. While the 1998 Act properly requires that regard must be had to the determinations of the Commission and the Committee of Ministers as a source of interpretation of the Convention rights, it is worth noting that the Court is now the only decision-making body in Strasbourg interpreting the Convention.

'TAKING INTO ACCOUNT'

4.4 During the Second Reading of the Bill in the House of Lords, the Lord Chancellor, Lord Irvine of Lairg, opened discussion on s 2 by explaining the following—

> '[Section] 2 requires courts in the United Kingdom to take account the decisions of the Convention institutions in Strasbourg in their consideration of Convention points which come before them. It is entirely appropriate that our courts should draw on the wealth of existing jurisprudence on the Convention.'[1]

---

[1]   HL 2R, 3 November 1997, col 1230.

4.5   In objecting to an Opposition amendment to substitute the word 'binding' for the phrase 'must take into account' during the Bill's consideration in Committee, Lord Irvine stated—

> '[On] . . . why we preferred in [section] 2(1) 'must take into account' rather than 'must be bound by'. Our courts must be free to develop human rights jurisprudence by taking into account European judgments and decisions, but they must also be free to distinguish them and to move out in new directions in relation to the whole area of human rights law.'[1]

[1]   HL Committee, 24 November 1997, col 835.

4.6   A more comprehensive explanation for the choice of the expression 'take into account' was given by Lord Irvine during the Report stage of the Bill, in response to an opposition amendment tabled to substitute the word 'binding'—

> '. . . the word 'binding' is the language of strict precedent but the Convention has no rule of precedent.
>
> . . .
>
> We take the view that the expression 'take into account' is clear enough. Should a United Kingdom court ever have a case before it which is a precise mirror of one that has been previously considered by the European Court of Human Rights, . . . it may be appropriate for it to apply the European court's findings directly to that case; but in real life cases are rarely as neat and tidy as that. The courts will often be faced with cases that involve factors perhaps specific to the United Kingdom which distinguish them from cases considered by the European Court.
>
> . . . it is important that our courts have the scope to apply that discretion so as to aid in the development of human rights law.
>
> There may also be occasions where it would be right for the United Kingdom courts to depart from a Strasbourg decision. We must remember that the interpretation of the Convention rights develops over the years. Circumstances may therefore arise in which a judgment given by the European Court of Human Rights decades ago contains pronouncements which it would not be appropriate to apply to the letter in the circumstances of today in a particular set of circumstances affecting this country. The Bill as currently drafted would allow our courts to use their common sense in applying the European court's judgment to such a case. We feel that to accept this amendment removes from the judges the flexibility and discretion that they require in developing human rights law.'[1]

[1]   HL Report, 19 January 1998, col 1270.

4.7   Whilst Lord Irvine was correct in stating that 'the Convention has no rule of precedent',[1] the Strasbourg Court has demonstrated through its case law that, whilst it does apply the doctrine of judicial precedent for the sake of certainty,[2] it views the Convention as 'a living instrument . . . to be interpreted in the light of present day conditions'.[3] Accordingly, where conditions have changed, the Court does not consider itself strictly bound by its previous decisions, particularly where it can be demonstrated that a pattern of commonly accepted standards has emerged in member States.[4] This approach is similar to that adopted by British judges in the development of the common law.

---

[1]   HL Report, 19 January 1998, col 1270.
[2]   See JG Merrills, 'The development of international law by the European Court of Human Rights', Manchester Press (2nd edn, 1993) particularly pp 12-16.
[3]   *Tyrer v United Kingdom* (1978) 2 EHRR 1 (para 31).
[4]   For example, in Tyrer *ibid* the Court, in finding a violation of Art 3 where birching of a juvenile in the Isle of Man had been permitted by domestic law, stated: 'In the case now before it the Court cannot be but influenced by the developments and commonly accepted standards in the penal policy of the member States of the Council of Europe in this field. Indeed, the Attorney-General for the Isle of Man mentioned that, for many years, the provisions of Manx legislation concerning judicial corporal punishment had been under review.' (para 31).

IMPORTANCE TO UK DECISION MAKING

4.8   Under Art 46(1) of the Convention, as amended by Protocol 11, the Court's decisions are binding on the Contracting States which 'undertake to abide by the final judgment of the Court in any case *to which they are parties*' [author's emphasis]. Thus, where the Court finds a violation against the UK, it is incumbent upon the Government to take steps to remedy the situation. In most cases this will entail amending or enacting primary legislation to remedy the defect under domestic law, and there are numerous occasions on which this has been done in response to an adverse finding in Strasbourg. For example, the Interception of Communications Act 1985 was enacted as a direct consequence of the Strasbourg Court's decision in *Malone v UK*[1] where the Court found that telephone tapping amounted to an adverse interference with an individual's right to privacy protected by Art 8 of the Convention. There has been a total of 11 changes to primary legislation as a result of adverse rulings in Strasbourg.

---

[1]   (1984) 7 EHRR 14.

4.9   Notably, s 2 of the Act does not restrict the 'account' which must be taken of Convention case law solely to those cases involving the UK. JG Merrills comments on the relevance of the UK courts having to take into account Strasbourg judgments and decisions concerning other States as follows—

> '. . . [E]ach ruling is not an isolated episode; it is also a contribution to the jurisprudence of the European Convention. In each case the Court is not just spelling out the obligations of the State which happens to be involved in the particular case. It is interpreting the Convention for all the States which are parties to it. Naturally, the main impact of the decision will usually be in the State immediately concerned, but every party to the Convention must stay abreast of developments. The common law, advancing from precedent to precedent, has a counterpart, then, in the developing law of the European Convention.'[1]

---

[1]   JG Merrills, 'The Development of International Law by the European Court of Human Rights', Manchester Press (2nd edn, 1993), p 12.

4.10 The importance behind the UK courts' obligation to take into account all the case law of the Strasbourg institutions is clear: such case law is the key to the interpretation of the Convention, regardless of whether the respondent State is the UK. An understanding of the Convention's extensive case law used to be considered the exclusive domain of those commonly termed 'international lawyers' or 'experts on human rights law'; however following the enactment of HRA 1998 the requirement of such knowledge has become more widespread. Accordingly, and to the possible chagrin of many solicitors and barristers, human rights law has been brought home.

Extent of requirement

4.11 Section 2(1) requires the courts to take into account Strasbourg case law in 'determining a question which has arisen in connection with a Convention right . . . so far as, in the opinion of the court or tribunal, it is relevant to the proceedings in which that question has arisen'.

4.12 There are two issues to consider here. First, the matter as to who should raise the 'question' and second, the issue of 'relevance'.

Raising a Convention question—whose duty: counsel or court?

4.13 The 1998 Act does not expressly place a duty on the court to raise a Convention question of its own volition. During Parliamentary debate Lord Mackay questioned the role of the courts in dealing with an unrepresented defendant who raises some general points based on Convention rights, proposing that '. . . if the [Strasbourg] jurisprudence is not cited, the judge is perfectly entitled to go ahead and decide the matter on the arguments advanced by the party defendant himself'. Lord Irvine replied—

> '. . . It is intended that Convention rights and values shall permeate the work of the courts at all levels. It is up to counsel to get themselves up to speed in that endeavour'.[1]

---

[1]   HL Committee, 18 November 1997, col 526.

4.14 Lord Irvine did concede that in cases where a defendant insists upon defending himself: '. . . there is a well recognised and honourable tradition in the courts of the judge giving the defendant the maximum assistance that he can.'[1] Lord Meston then asked: 'Will the noble and learned Lord also agree that there is a tradition that prosecuting counsel should assist the court in those circumstances?' to which Lord Irvine confirmed, 'yes'.[2]

---

[1]   HL Committee, 18 November 1997, col 526.
[2]   Ibid, col 527.

4.15 In the same debate Lord Irvine had stated that whilst the plans for judicial training were proceeding under the auspices of the Judicial Studies Board—

> 'Counsel should not be spoon-fed. It is the duty of counsel to research their case and, if they have a Convention point which they desire to

raise, they must equip themselves to do so and gain copies of any relevant reports that they desire to draw to the attention of the court. It is not the function of the State to do counsel's research for him.'[1]

---

[1] HL Committee, 18 November 1997, col 526.

4.16 While a duty may lie with counsel to raise a question of Convention rights before the court where appropriate to do so, and to provide substance for this legal argument, the repercussions for a court in failing to recognise or to raise a Convention point of its own volition, which may have been missed by counsel, could be serious. A court or tribunal is a public authority by virtue of s 6(3)(a) of the 1998 Act, which makes it unlawful for either to act in any manner which is incompatible with a Convention right. An 'act' includes an omission, and perhaps even an unintentional failure by a public authority to act in compliance with an individual's Convention rights.[1] A court which fails to take into account relevant Strasbourg case-law determining any question relating to an individual's Convention rights may find itself subject to proceedings for breach of HRA 1998, s 6 regardless of whether or not a question concerning a Convention point was raised before the court. It will be no defence to a claim for breach of s 6 for a court to say that no Convention question was raised before the Bench. The importance of the court clerk's knowledge of the Convention and its case law, particularly in magistrates' court proceedings before a lay Bench, is undeniable.

---

[1] See, for example, Mike O'Brien, Parliamentary Under-Secretary of State for the Home Department, HC Committee, 24 June 1998, col 1097, see para 8.19 below.

4.17 A simple omission by a court to regard Strasbourg case law may render its actions unlawful due to non-compliance with the Convention. Although damages may not be awarded in respect of a judicial act done in good faith (except so far as to compensate a person to the extent required by Art 5(5)),[1] alternative remedies may exist where the case is heard before a criminal court which failed to act compatibly with the Convention. For example, a defendant's case may be quashed on appeal.

---

[1] See further, paras 11.3–11.5.

4.18 Under the 1998 Act, courts are not bound by the determinations emanating from Strasbourg. Where such case law is 'relevant to the proceedings', the Court must take it into account under s 2(1). The duty to raise a Convention point is one which may be easily shared by counsel and the court, or uneasily, as regards the court, rest upon counsel alone.

The issue of relevant case law

4.19 The failure to include Art 13 as an express 'Convention right' in HRA 1998, s 1, is discussed at paras 3.13–3.18. It is mentioned here in the context of whether it is only the case law pertaining to the Convention rights listed in s 1(1) which may be 'relevant' under s 1(2), or whether other Convention rights unenumerated in the Act, such as Art 13 and its case law, may also be 'relevant' and hence subject to consideration by the court.

4.20 Lord Lester asked the following question of Lord Irvine, during the Committee stage of the Bill in the House of Lords—

> '. . . Is it the intention of the Government that the courts should not be entitled to have regard to Article 13 and the case law of the Strasbourg Court on that Article in cases where it would otherwise be relevant?'[1]

In response Lord Irvine stated that '. . . the courts may have regard to Article 13.'[2]

---

[1]   HL Committee, 18 November 1997, col 476.
[2]   Ibid, col 477.

4.21 It is however arguable that while a court must take into account relevant Strasbourg case law concerning the 'Convention rights' as defined in s 1(1), the court does not bear the same duty under HRA 1998 concerning Art 13. This will also be true of human rights case law from other international jurisdictions such as New Zealand or Canada which may be argued before the domestic courts to reinforce an argument on a Convention point. Although in both general and specific terms such case law might be 'relevant' to the proceedings, the extent of this relevancy is not fixed to a binding obligation by the courts to take it into account. It may be simply a matter of discretion for the courts to have regard to such case law where Convention arguments are raised, even if, in order for courts to act effectively to protect the Convention rights, it may be essential to consider such determinations where relevant to the proceedings.

THE CONTRIBUTION OF BRITISH JUDGES

4.22 One issue reiterated by the Government during the passage of the Human Rights Bill through Parliament was the potential contribution by UK judges to the interpretation of the Convention. By giving the Convention rights 'further effect' and allowing them to be directly justiciable before domestic courts, UK judges will be able to stamp a 'British hallmark' on cases where Convention rights are raised.

4.23 Prior to HRA 1998, the Convention was not itself enforceable, and could only be used to aid the enforcement of domestic legislation and the common law. Judges were not empowered to rule in favour of Convention rights, nor to read into legislation such rights except where ambiguity existed on the face of such legislation.[1] British judges were therefore not delivering judgments based on hearing fully argued Convention points in cases heard before the domestic courts. Such judgments would have applied to the facts the vital principles of interpretation of the Convention, such as proportionality and the necessity of restrictions by the State in a democratic society. Consequently, in applications dealt with by the Commission and cases considered by the Court where violations by the UK were alleged, the Strasbourg institutions would have benefited from hearing such judgments. Instead the judgments laid before the Commission and Court did not include any analysis of the Convention or its interpretation.

---

[1]   See for example *R v Secretary of State for the Home Department ex p Brind* [1991] AC 696, 747 per Lord Bridge 'the Courts . . . have no power to enforce Convention rights directly'. This case has now been overruled by the enactment of HRA 1998.

4.24 It is arguable that as a consequence the UK could not benefit fully from the application of the margin of appreciation doctrine, afforded to other States in certain areas of Convention application by the Strasbourg Commission and Court.[1] The Commission and Court were able to consider written or oral representations on the interpretation of the Convention to UK law only when provided by parties after a case was accepted for consideration in Strasbourg. This situation was unsatisfactory, particularly as the Commission was being forced to deal with a far higher percentage of applications from UK citizens than any other State Party. Furthermore, and arguably, the British Government faced an uphill battle to persuade the Commission and Court that domestic law complied with the Convention without the benefit of reasoned judgments on Convention points by the British judiciary. The Strasbourg institutions were placed in the position of being the primary decision makers on Convention issues in UK cases, not in the role of reviewing bodies as intended by the Convention draftsmen.

---

[1] By this the Court has accepted that States have a certain degree of discretion to determine the compatibility of their conduct with the requirements of the Convention. This discretion is particularly applicable in cases concerning rights protected by Arts 8–11 of the Convention, which provide circumstances in which State interference may be permissible. See *Handyside v UK* (1976) 1 EHRR 737. The doctrine of margin of appreciation does not apply to domestic consideration of Convention issues under HRA 1998 because its role is limited to cases heard before the Strasbourg Court, which attempts to supervise the enforcement of the Convention in 41 Contracting States and adopts the margin of appreciation to assist this.

4.25 The importance of the interpretative obligation imposed upon the courts by virtue of s 2 was underlined by Mike O'Brien during Second Reading in the House of Commons—

> 'Enabling our courts to take account of the Convention is about more than reaching quicker decisions. It will mean that the judges of a domestic court can consider all the issues relevant to a case before them. They will no longer have to put out of their mind Convention arguments that might be relevant to the case, but which they are currently debarred from considering. Therefore, the Bill will change the approach that the courts adopt to Convention case.

> The present situation is wholly unsatisfactory for the courts and for individuals. It is artificial to cordon off a set of rights and make them the exclusive preserve of the Court in Strasbourg. It leads to frustration and it impedes effective justice.

> . . .

> [On worries] about politicisation. I consider that our judges must be able to bring their knowledge of the United Kingdom's traditions and practices to bear on the cases that come before them. They will be able to interpret the Convention rights in ways sensitive to the specific circumstances that will apply in this country. The rights under the Convention will become interwoven with our laws.

> The Strasbourg Court recognises that domestic courts have the primary role to play in protecting individuals' rights under the Convention. The proper role of the Strasbourg Court is to act as a backstop but, at present, the Strasbourg institutions are often placed in the front line, as the first bodies to consider issues arising under the Convention. That serves no one's interest.

We already accept the judgments of a European body in respect of the Convention, and have amended our laws many times in response to its findings. Therefore we already adapt our laws in the light of Convention rights. Incorporation will mean, however, that the United Kingdom courts can assist in shaping those rights in a manner sensitive to our country's ways. At present they cannot. Moreover, at a time when the United Kingdom has committed a total of 50 violations of the Convention, it smacks of complacency to say that we have nothing to learn by giving effect to Convention rights in our law.'[1]

---

[1]   HC 2R, 16 February 1998, cols 858, 859.

RULES

4.26 HRA 1998, s 2(2) provides for rules to be made by the relevant minister determining the manner in which evidence of the Strasbourg case law is to be presented in court proceedings. Such rules have yet to be finalised, but are expected in early 2000 (see para 19.2).

5 Interpretation of legislation

OBLIGATIONS

5.1   Under s 3(1) *'so far as it is possible to do so,* primary legislation and subordinate legislation *must be read and given effect* in a way which is compatible with the Convention rights' [author's emphasis]. The obligation extends to both current and future primary and secondary legislation (s 3(2)(a): see paras 1.12–1.17).

5.2   As explained by the Lord Chancellor, Lord Irvine of Lairg, during Second Reading in the House of Lords—

> '[Section] 3 provides that legislation, whenever enacted must as far as possible be read and given effect in a way which is compatible with the Convention rights. This will ensure that, if it is possible to interpret a statute in two ways—one compatible with the Convention and one not—the courts will always chose the interpretation which is compatible. In practice, this will prove a strong form of incorporation.'[1]

---

[1]   HL 2R, 3 November 1997, col 1230.

5.3   The wording of s 3(1) raises two points for consideration, the meaning of the phrase 'so far as it is possible' and the requirement that legislation 'must be read and given effect'.

'SO FAR AS IT IS POSSIBLE TO DO SO'

5.4   Those who participated in the Parliamentary debates concerning the wording of s 3(1) sought to establish what was meant by the words 'so far as possible' and indeed how the new obligation placed upon the courts would differ from the existing methods of interpretation. In the view of Lord Cooke of Thorndon—

> 'The clause will require a very different approach to interpretation from that to which United Kingdom courts are accustomed. Traditionally, the search has been for the true meaning; now it will be for a possible meaning that would prevent the making of a declaration of incompatibility.
>
> . . .
>
> The shift of the criterion to a search for possible compatible meanings will confront the courts with delicate responsibilities . . . In effect, the courts are being asked to solve . . . problems [of interpretation] by applying a rebuttable presumption in favour of the Convention rights.'[1]

---

[1]   HL 2R, 3 November 1997, col 1272.

5.5   Lord Lester spoke of the link between the 'very strong wording' of the provision and the need to safeguard Convention principles—

> 'The Bill will not empower our courts to strike down legislation which it is impossible to read in accordance with Convention rights. But the command by Parliament in the Bill to the courts to read them in that way,
>
> 'so far as possible'
>
> represents very strong wording. The courts will no doubt strive as far as is judicially possible to save legislation from having to be declared incompatible, and hence, to be amended by future further legislation. The courts will do so by construing existing and future legislation as intended to provide the necessary safeguards to ensure fairness, proportionality and legal certainty as required by the Convention.'[1]

---

[1]   HL 2R, 3 November 1997, col 1240.

A duty to contort the law?

5.6   Lord Irvine and the Home Secretary, Jack Straw, sought to allay fears that the courts might be induced by the wording of s 3(1) to contort the true meaning of legislation in order to make incompatible legislation compatible. Lord Irvine stated that—

> 'The word 'possible' is the plainest means that we can devise for simply asking the courts to find the construction consistent with the intentions of Parliament and the wording of legislation which is nearest to the Convention rights . . . we want the courts to construe statutes so that they bear a meaning that is consistent with the Convention whenever that is possible according to the language of the statutes but not when it is impossible to achieve that. More generally, we proceed on the basis that Parliament, at least post-ratification of the Convention, must be deemed to have intended its statutes to be compatible with the Convention to which the United Kingdom is bound, and that courts should hold that that deemed general intention has not been carried successfully into effect only where it is impossible to construe a statute as having that effect.'[1]

Jack Straw stated—

> 'In many cases, particularly in respect of statutory interpretation, the whole task of the court is not to make up the law, but to say what it means where that is not clear or where its application in particular circumstances is not clear. The courts are well versed in the interpretation of the law and of Parliament's intention . . . it is not our intention that the courts, in applying what is now [section] 3, should contort the meaning of the words to produce implausible or incredible meanings.'[2]

---

[1]   HL Committee, 18 November 1997, col 535. See also commentary on HRA 1998, s 19—Statements of Compatibility, at Ch 18.

[2]   HC Committee, 3 June 1998, col 422.

5.7   Therefore the courts should find legislation compatible with the Convention whenever it is possible to do so, and the plain meaning of the word 'possible' ought to be adopted by the court during its deliberations. The aim is not to distort the true meaning of the legislation in question. As provided by HRA 1998, s 4, the opportunity to make a declaration of incompatibility exists where the court finds it impossible to construe legislation in line with the Convention rights.[1]

---

[1]   See commentary to HRA 1998, s 4 at Ch 6.

TO READ AND GIVE EFFECT

5.8   As Lord Cooke pointed out—

'. . . if a national court has made a declaration of incompatibility and expeditious remedial steps have not followed, will not that state of affairs amount to a plain invitation to a journey to Strasbourg? After all, as was pointed out, the European Court of Human Rights retains all its power and can always have the last word. That in itself may well be a strong incentive for adopting compatible interpretations in this jurisdiction.'[1]

---

[1]   HL 2R, 3 November 1997, col 1272.

5.9   The Government expects that in 99% of all cases[1] the courts will find that the legislation is compatible with the Convention. However, it remains to be seen whether this is a realistic expectation. There will invariably be some 'hard' cases brought to court where it will be more difficult for the judges to decide which of the two options available to them they should adopt, either to find it is possible to interpret the legislation compatibly with the Convention or find it impossible to do so. In such cases Lord Irvine provided some indications as to by what principles judges might be guided—

'We want the courts to strive to find an interpretation of legislation which is consistent with Convention rights *so far as the language of the legislation allows* and only in the last resort to conclude that the legislation is simply incompatible with them' [author's emphasis].[2]

---

[1]   HL 3R, 5 February 1998, col 840.
[2]   HL Committee, 18 November 1997, col 535.

5.10 Lord Irvine emphasised that 'The Convention rights are the magnetic north and the needle of judicial interpretation will swing towards them'.[1]

---

[1]   HL 3R, 5 February 1998, col 840.

5.11 These are compelling propositions and ought to be considered by every judge adjudicating a Convention point. For the first time, the onus of judicial interpretation will be on securing to everyone in the UK the human rights contained within the Convention which are now protected by HRA 1998. If the courts are also obliged to act effectively to protect these rights, as is suggested by the words 'given effect' in s 3(1), they must exercise their interpretative powers to give effect to the Convention rights, even if to do so requires a departure from established precedent. Wherever it is possible to do so, legislation must be read and given effect in a manner which upholds an individual's Convention rights. Thus, while considering Convention rights and the 'magnetic north' the courts may find the wording of the legislation allows them enough scope to 'read in' fundamental rights absent from legislation, or to devise new methods of interpreting legislation to give effect to Convention rights.

5.12 As the Lord Chief Justice, Lord Bingham of Cornhill, stated during the Second Reading of the Bill in the House of Lords—

> 'It seems to me highly desirable that we in the United Kingdom should help to mould the law by which we are governed in this area . . . I think . . . that British judges have a significant contribution to make in the development of the law of human rights. It is a contribution which so far we have not been permitted to make . . . also . . . when cases from this country reach Strasbourg, as on occasion they will do, the court will have the benefit of a considered judgment by a British judge on the point at issue.'[1]

---

[1]   HL 2R, 3 November 1997, col 1245.

5.13 Lord Bingham raised an important point. Some cases will still arrive before the Strasbourg Court, and if the judgments of the UK courts are to withstand such scrutiny, they must not be flawed by false reasoning. The enactment of HRA 1998 will allow British judges a prime and public opportunity to make significant contributions to human rights law.

THE APPLICATION OF s 3(1): WHOSE OBLIGATION?

5.14 While all relevant discussions in Parliament centred on the courts' obligation to read and give effect to legislation so far as it is possible to do so, the application of s 3(1) is not so limited. Specific reference to a court or a tribunal or to any other body is absent from the wording of the section. It may be concluded therefore that the obligation under s 3(1) is far-reaching and arguably may encroach upon any body which has the authority to read and give effect to legislation. Without further assistance from the Parliamentary debates it is at least arguable at this preliminary stage that all public bodies and that even private bodies may be so bound. What is clear, however, is that a court's obligation under s 3(1) will extend to proceedings between private litigants and will not simply depend upon a public authority being party to proceedings.

THE CONTINUING FORCE OF INCOMPATIBLE LEGISLATION

5.15 As Lord Irvine stated—

> 'The [Act] does not allow the courts to set aside or ignore Acts of Parliament. [Section] 3 preserves the effect of primary legislation which is incompatible with the Convention. It does the same for secondary legislation where it is inevitably incompatible because of the terms of the parent statute'.[1]

1   HL 2R, 3 November 1997, col 1230.

5.16 Where the domestic courts are unable to declare that primary legislation is compatible with the Convention, HRA 1998, s 3(2)(b) provides that this 'does not affect the validity, continuing operation or enforcement of any incompatible primary legislation'. This preserves the status quo in relation to the power of the courts concerning primary legislation prior to HRA 1998. The courts do not at present, nor will they once HRA 1998 enters into force, have the power to quash Acts of Parliament.[2]

1   See paras 6.9, 6.10 for an explanation of the situation concerning Acts of the Scottish Parliament.

5.17 As Lord Irvine stated, the courts do not have the power 'to set aside or ignore Acts of Parliament'[1] under HRA 1998. Jack Straw reiterated this during Committee in the House of Commons—

> 'Consistent with maintaining parliamentary sovereignty, [section] 3 . . . provides that if a provision of primary legislation cannot be interpreted compatibly with the Convention rights, that legislation will continue to have force and effect.'[2]

Lord Irvine also explained that '. . . if statutes are held incompatible on Convention grounds, then it is for Parliament to remedy that'.[3]

1   HL 2R, 3 November 1997, col 1230.
2   HC 2R, 16 February 1998, col 780.
3   HL Committee, 18 November 1998, col 522.

STRIKING DOWN SUBORDINATE LEGISLATION

5.18 The courts have existing powers to strike down subordinate legislation and they may continue to exercise such powers under the 1998 Act, providing the parent statute is not primary legislation which prevents removal of the incompatibility with the Convention rights (s 3(2)(c)). In such cases, the incompatible subordinate legislation will continue to have force. Jack Straw explained—

> '. . . the courts already have power to strike down subordinate legislation, and they do so with some regularity. If they feel that a statutory instrument has been introduced in a way that is ultra vires the primary legislation, they can do so . . . it seemed to us that, as that power was already there, it would be very odd not to continue to allow courts to strike down subordinate legislation if it was incompatible with the Bill.
>
> In a sense, that does not affect the sovereignty of Parliament, because it is open to Ministers to try to put the subordinate legislation right by simply introducing further regulations. That happens quite often . . . '[1]

1   HC Committee, 24 June 1998, col 1128.

6 Declarations of incompatibility

6.1   Section 4 provides that a court[1] may make a declaration of incompatibility where a provision of primary or subordinate legislation is found to be incompatible with the Convention rights. As the Lord Chancellor, Lord Irvine of Lairg, explained during Second Reading in the House of Lords—

> 'In the very rare cases where the higher courts will find it impossible to read and give effect to any statute in a way which is compatible with Convention rights, they will be able to make a declaration of incompatibility.'[2]

---

1   For discussion on courts empowered to make declarations of incompatibility, see para 6.5 below.
2   HL 2R, 3 November 1997, col 582.

Primary legislation

6.2   In any proceedings where the court, having considered the compatibility of a provision of primary legislation with a Convention right (s 4(1)), nonetheless finds it impossible to read the provision in a way which is compatible with that right, s 4(2) provides that 'if the court is satisfied that the provision is incompatible with a Convention right, it *may* make a declaration of that incompatibility' [author's emphasis] (see para 6.4).

Subordinate legislation

6.3   In any proceedings where the court is determining whether a provision of subordinate legislation made in the exercise of a power conferred by primary legislation is compatible with a Convention right (s 4(3)) it may make a declaration of incompatibility under s 4(4). The court must be satisfied that the provision is incompatible with a Convention right (s 4(4)(a)), and that, disregarding any possibility of revocation, the parent statute prevents removal of the incompatibility. Section 4 provides a court with a 'discretion' and not an obligation to issue a declaration of incompatibility.

DISCRETION TO MAKE A DECLARATION OF INCOMPATIBILITY

6.4   The use of the phrase 'may make a declaration of that incompatibility' introduces a new discretion to the process of judicial reasoning. During the House of Lords consideration of the Bill in Committee Lord Irvine explained the reason for the choice of the word 'may'—

> 'The reason [section] 4 only confers a discretion is in part that in our domestic law a declaration is generally a discretionary remedy. A [section] 4 declaration has no operative or coercive effect and in

particular does not prevent either party relying on, or the courts enforcing, the law in question unless and until changed by Parliament.

The courts may, therefore, not wish to make a declaration of incompatibility in all cases. It is possible that the facts of particular cases may suggest that legislation as it is applied in that case is incompatible with the Convention, but there may be reasons peculiar to the particular case why the legislation should not be declared incompatible on the occasion when the court could be free to do that.

. . . I certainly would expect courts generally to make declarations of incompatibility when they find an Act to be incompatible with the Convention. However, we do not wish to deny them a discretion not to do so because of the particular circumstances of any case.

. . . [for example] . . . there might be an alternative statutory appeal route which the court might think it preferable to follow, or there might be any other procedure which the court in its discretion thought the applicant should exhaust before seeking a declaration which would then put Parliament under pressure to follow a remedial route.

. . . it appears to me to be sensible to leave the courts a discretion . . . . I well recognise that in the great majority of cases courts would want to make declarations of incompatibility, where that was appropriate.'[1]

---

[1]   HL Committee, 18 November 1997, col 546.

RELEVANT COURTS

6.5   Section 4(5) defines the reference to a 'court' for the purposes of s 4 as the following—
— the House of Lords (s 4(5)(a));
— the Judicial Committee of the Privy Council (s 4(5)(b));
— the Courts-Martial Appeal Court (s 4(5)(c));
— the High Court of Justiciary in Scotland, when sitting other than as a trial court or the Court of Session (s 4(5)(d)); and
— the High Court and Court of Appeal in England and Wales or Northern Ireland (s 4(5)(e)).

6.6   The discretion to grant a declaration of incompatibility applies to 'any proceedings' where the compatibility of primary and subordinate legislation is being determined by any of these higher courts (s 4(1) and (3) respectively).

6.7   Absent from the list of courts are criminal courts, most notably the Central Criminal Court ie, the Old Bailey. This reasoning for this reflected the policy behind HRA 1998 concerning criminal cases—

'. . . judges who preside over criminal trials should not have the power to make declarations of incompatibility . . . we do not believe that trials should be upset, or potentially upset, by declarations of incompatibility that may go to the very foundations of the prosecution.'[1]

---

[1]   Lord Irvine, HL Committee, 18 November 1997, col 551.

6.8   Instead, the higher courts listed in s 4(5) will be able to make declarations of incompatibility depending on their competence in civil and criminal cases.

DECLARATIONS OF INCOMPATIBILITY IN SCOTLAND

6.9   In Scotland, only the High Court of Justiciary, when sitting other than as a trial court or the Court of Session, has competence under s 4 to issue declarations of incompatibility in Scotland in relation to primary or secondary legislation of the Parliament. However, the legislative competence of the Scottish Parliament is limited, inter alia, to legislating in compliance with any of the Convention rights (Scotland Act 1998, s 28). Furthermore, an Act of the Scottish Parliament is not law so far as any provision contained within it is incompatible with any of the Convention rights (s 29(2)).

6.10   Desmond Browne (Kilmarnock and Loudoun) explained the link between the Scotland Act 1998 and the Human Rights Act 1998—

'The point at which the Scotland [Act] and the Human Rights [Act] intersect has implications for Scotland and the UK. In the words of the Scottish Human Rights Centre—

'Together they represent an historical milestone in enabling Scotland to begin to develop a modern human rights agenda'.

Taken together, the [Acts] enable a High Court and Court of Session to strike down any Act of the Scottish Parliament or action of a Scottish Minister which is incompatible with the European Convention on human rights. Nevertheless the UK Parliament's claim of absolute sovereignty is recognised; and the superior courts in Scotland, as in England and Wales, will be able to make an open declaration of incompatibility only in relation to primary legislation of this Parliament—although they will continue, as they do so now on both sides of the border, to be able to declare secondary legislation ultra vires.

That difference quite properly reflects a devolution. Both jurisdictions have different constitutional traditions and differing forms of incorporation are consistent with each.'[1]

---

[1]   HC 2R, 16 February 1998, col 832.

THE CONTINUING FORCE OF INCOMPATIBLE LEGISLATION

6.11   If a court makes a declaration of incompatibility under either s 4(2) (primary legislation) or under s 4(4) (subordinate legislation), s 4(6) provides that the incompatible provision shall remain in force and further provides that the declaration is not binding on the parties to the proceedings in which it is made.

6.12 The clarity of the language of s 4(6) has been described by the Home Secretary, Jack Straw, as 'the default setting', by which confusion as to the effect of a declaration of incompatibility on existing legislation is avoided. Jack Straw explained—

> '[Section] 4(6) is clear . . . In a judicial and political sense, the status quo ante would apply. Then, obviously, the Government would have to consider, and in most cases they would consider the position pretty rapidly. No time limit is set down, but the reverse could not apply. We could not, for example, say that the declaration of incompatibility would have force unless or until the Government said the reverse. That would create considerable uncertainty . . .'[1]

---

[1]   HC Report, 21 October 1998, col 1306.

6.13 During Second Reading of the Bill in the House of Commons Jack Straw had stated—

> 'A declaration of incompatibility will not affect the continuing validity of the legislation in question. That would be contrary to the principle of the Bill. However, it would be a clear signal to the Government and Parliament that, in the court's view, a provision of legislation does not conform to the standards of the Convention . . . it is likely that the Government and Parliament would wish to respond to such a situation and would do so rapidly.'[1]

---

[1]   HC 2R, 16 February 1998, col 780.

6.14 The White Paper had been more certain—'A declaration . . . will almost certainly prompt the Government and Parliament to change the law.'[1]

---

[1]   'Rights Brought Home: The Human Rights Bill', Cm 3782 (1997), para 2.10.

THE EFFECT OF A DECLARATION OF INCOMPATIBILITY

6.15 What effect then, if any, does a declaration of incompatibility have? In the opinion of Lord Lester—

> 'Every declaration of incompatibility will represent a systemic failure, as our statute book is already made to comply with our Convention obligations. A declaration of incompatibility will also be highly inconvenient because it will mean that our courts are unable to provide an effective judicial remedy and that the inconsistency will have to be remedied by government and Parliament under the special fast-track legislative procedure; or, if not, it will have to be remedied by the overburdened European Court of Human Rights.'[1]

---

[1]   HL 2R, 3 November 1997, col 1240.

6.16 The purpose of the declaration of incompatibility may then be to bring to the Government's attention the prohibitive nature of certain pieces of legislation which restrict the courts in giving effect to the Convention rights. The 'threat' of cases going to Strasbourg will remain unless and until the Government decides to make amendments to the offending legislation by passing a remedial order or indeed a full amending Bill. Parliament does, however, remain free and sovereign in the face of a declaration of incompatibility to choose whether to do so (see Ch 12 on remedial actions and orders).

DECLARATIONS OF INCOMPATIBILITY AND PARLIAMENTARY SOVEREIGNTY

6.17 The use of declarations of incompatibility where there is incompatible legislation which cannot be resolved by judicial interpretation under Art 3 may be described as a novel method by which Parliamentary sovereignty is retained. Only Parliament may decide whether to change the law in such circumstances and the 1998 Act does not permit the doctrine of implied repeal to operate where legislation is found by the courts to be incompatible. Robert Maclennan commented on this feature of the Bill during the Parliamentary debates—

> ' . . . unlike the European Communities Act 1972 . . . the Bill does not give primacy to treaty rights where there is a provision in this Parliament's legislation that is incompatible with a Convention right. In their endeavour to ensure the supremacy of Parliament, the Government have followed a novel course. They have provided only that the courts may make a declaration of incompatibility. They have eschewed the more normal statutory interpretation that there has been an implied repeal if Parliament has enacted a measure subsequently. As a result of the form in which the measure is couched, it falls to Parliament to decide whether to safeguard the Convention right by the means set out in [section] 10 [and Schedule 2].'

> . . . Far from introducing . . . an 'incompatible constitutional framework', the Bill is deferential to the sensitivities of the judiciary about being given an overriding constitutional power.'[1]

It is important to note that where a court is considering whether to grant a declaration of incompatibility under s 4 of the Act, the Crown is provided by s 5 with the right to intervene as a party to those proceedings.[2]

---

1   HC 2R, 16 February 1998, col 806.
2   See Ch 7 for a discussion of s 5.

7 The right of the Crown to intervene

THE RIGHTS OF THE CROWN

7.1 As the Lord Chancellor, Lord Irvine of Lairg, explained during the Second Reading in the House of Lords—

> '[Section] 4 provides for the rare cases where the courts may have to make declarations of incompatibility. Such declarations are serious. That is why [section] 5 gives the Crown the right to have notice of any case where a court is considering making a declaration of incompatibility and the right to be joined as a party to the proceedings, so that it can make representations on the point.'[1]

---

[1]   HL 2R, 3 November 1997, col 1231.

NOTICE TO THE CROWN AND JOINDER

7.2   Section 5(1) provides that 'where a court is considering whether to make a declaration of incompatibility, the Crown is entitled to notice in accordance with rules of court'.[1] Further to such notice being given by the court, s 5(2) provides that designated persons and bodies are entitled, upon giving notice in accordance with the rules of court, to be joined as a party to those proceedings. Those designated as eligible to be joined are—

(a) a Minister of the Crown or a person nominated by him (s 5(2)(a));
(b) a member of the Scottish executive (s 5(2)(b));
(c) a Northern Ireland Minister (s 5(2)(c));
(d) a Northern Ireland department (s 5(2)(d)).

Notice to be joined may be given at any stage of the proceedings (s 5(3)).

---

[1]   These had not yet been drafted by the time this book went to print.

APPEAL AGAINST DECLARATIONS OF INCOMPATIBILITY IN CRIMINAL CASES

7.3   In criminal proceedings, including proceedings before the Courts-Martial Appeal Court (s 5(5)), s 5(4) provides that where a declaration of incompatibility is made by a court, and where a person has been joined to the proceedings in accordance with s 5(2), that person is entitled to appeal against the declaration, subject to leave being granted, to the House of Lords.

7.4   Notably, the entitlement to appeal under HRA 1998, s 5(4) is restricted to criminal proceedings heard in England and Wales. It does not apply to criminal proceedings heard before the Scottish courts because in such cases there is no pre-existing right of appeal to the House of Lords.

THE RIGHT TO BE JOINED

7.5   The inclusion of s 5 is linked to the potential impact that a declaration of incompatibility will have on the Crown, including the possibility of remedial orders initiated by the relevant Minister under HRA 1998, s 10, Sch 2 (see Ch 12). For this reason it was felt necessary to permit intervention by the Crown before a declaration is made, and for the Government representative most informed about the incompatible legislation in question to make representations to the court during its considerations. An opportunity unfortunately missed was to include within s 5 a discretion of the court to invite or to grant leave to permit intervention by other interested parties such as representative groups in the appropriate circumstances, as is permitted when a case is before the consideration of the Strasbourg Court.[1]

---

[1]   See Art 36(2) of the Convention: 'The President of the Court may, in the interest of the proper administration of justice, invite any High Contracting Party which is not a party to the proceedings *or any person concerned who is not the applicant* to submit written comments or to take part in hearings.' [author's emphasis]. See also Rules of Procedure of the European Court of Human Rights, particularly Rule 42 (Measures for taking evidence) and Rule 61 (Third-party intervention).

JOINDER OF NOMINEES

7.6   Discussion during the Bill's passage through Parliament questioned the use of the phrase 'a Minister of the Crown (or a person nominated by him)' in s 5(2)(a), in particular who this nominee might be. Lord Irvine explained—

> '[Section] 5(2) entitles a Minister of the Crown or a person nominated by a Minister of the Crown to be joined as a party to the proceedings where a court is considering making a declaration of incompatibility . . . It appears to us that it will, or may in some cases, be more appropriate for a person nominated by a Minister of the Crown rather than a Minister to be joined as a party to the proceedings.
>
> That is true, for example, in relation to private Acts or to measures of the Church Assembly or to measures of the General Synod or to regulators of public utilities or to the Director General of Fair Trading, to name but a few.
>
> . . .
>
> It is intended that a person other than a Minister of the Crown or lawyer acting for a Minister of the Crown could be joined as a party to the proceedings if thought by the Minister of the Crown to be more appropriate because that would offer greater assistance to the court in relation to the legislation under consideration.[1]

---

[1]   HL Committee, 18 November 1997, cols 555, 556.

THE COST OF THE CROWN'S INTERVENTION

7.7   Lord Henley, during the First Day of Committee in the House of Lords, moved for an amendment suggesting that the Crown should pay its own costs of being joined to the proceedings. Lord Lester felt some sympathy with this amendment, by reason of the deterrent effect of costs orders—

> 'Obviously it would normally be dealt with as a matter of discretion by the courts, but it seems to me that it would be right to put the matter beyond doubt in the way that this amendment suggests so that there is no sword of Damocles hanging over the head of the litigant that if there is a Crown intervention, then there may be liability for his costs, the respondent's costs and the Crown's costs as well.'[1]

---

[1]   HL Committee, 18 November 1998, col 557.

7.8   The Government, however, remained unpersuaded. Lord Williams of Mostyn, Under-Secretary of State at the Home Office, replied—

> 'As the Committee will be aware, the courts, in particular the higher courts to which this clause is relevant, already have considerable discretion to make orders for costs affecting both parties and non-parties to litigation . . . In relation to civil cases in the High Court and the Court of Appeal, Section 51(3) of the Supreme Court Act 1981 states that,
>
> 'the Court shall have full power to determine by whom and to what extent the costs are to be paid.'
>
> Various well known provisions on the award of costs in criminal cases are contained in the Prosecution of Offences Act 1985.
>
> I suggest, with great respect, that there are good reasons why the allocation of costs should be left to the judges' discretion. The important point, among others, is that the court in question has heard the case fully; it knows all the relevant facts and it has the benefit of submission from counsel for all parties. There are many factors which judges would properly want to take into account when assessing how costs should be allocated. This is not intended to be an exhaustive list, but these would include whether the case put forward by the party seeking the declaration had any substantive merit . . . Another question could be: was there any wider public interest in the case? That ought to be a matter affecting the judge when he decides on the costs order. He would probably want legitimately in this area to consider the financial position of the applicant. That is not, of course, a strong aspect of judicial discretion in costs orders in the generality of cases, but it might—if a particular judge thought it appropriate—be relevant in this class of case. What is the outcome of the case? Is a declaration of incompatibility . . . ultimately awarded? How many other members of the public might be affected? What is the ambit of the legislative component which is subject to a declaration of incompatibility? All those are subtle questions that judges ought to balance rather than being disqualified from carrying out that balance simply by the brutality of this present amendment.'[1]

---

[1]   HL Committee, 18 November 1998, col 557.

7.9   Lord Williams did concede, however, that circumstances may exist where a court may be justified in ordering costs against the Crown for intervening—

> 'There are likely to be cases—one recognises this—where the Crown would be required to meet its own costs. For instance, a tribunal might feel that the point behind the declaration of incompatibility was so plain that the Minister in question had behaved irrationally or unreasonably in contesting the matter. It might be thought that the interest of the Crown was so marginal that the relevant Minister might perhaps never have applied to be joined, on the powers given to him in the Bill . . . It may even be that the Crown would have to meet the costs of other parties. There might be some cases where neither would be appropriate.'[1]

---

[1]   HL Committee, 18 November 1998, col 559.

A PUBLIC FUND FOR IMPORTANT CASES

7.10 During the Second Reading in the House of Lords, Lord Williams stated that Lord Irvine would give serious consideration to proposals to create a special fund for cases concerning matters of public interest.[1] Later, during Committee, Lord Williams indicated that Lord Irvine had pledged to establish a fund which was to be devoted to a certain class of case—litigants who bring a strong arguable case on a genuine issue of public importance.[2]

---

[1]   HL 2R, 3 November 1997, col 1308.
[2]   HL Committee, 18 November 1998, col 560.

8 Acts of public authorities

PUBLIC AUTHORITIES v CONVENTION RIGHTS

8.1   Under s 6(1), 'it is unlawful for a public authority to act in a way which is incompatible with a Convention right'. During Committee in the House of Lords, the Lord Chancellor, Lord Irvine of Lairg, discussed the prohibition contained within s 6(1)—

> '[Section] 6(1) refers to a 'public authority' without defining the term. In many cases it will be obvious to the courts that they will be dealing with a public authority. In respect of government departments, for example, or police officers, or prison officers, or immigration officers, or local authorities, there can be no doubt that the body in question is a public authority. Any clear case of that kind comes in under [section] 6(1); and it is then unlawful for the authority to act in a way which is incompatible with one or more of the Convention rights. In such cases, the prohibition applies in respect of all their acts, public and private. There is no exemption for private acts such as is conferred by [section] 6(5) in relation to [section 6(3)(b)].
>
> [Section 6(3)(b)] provides further assistance on the meaning of public authority. It provides that 'public authority' includes,
>
> 'any person certain of whose functions are functions of a public nature'.
>
> That provision is there to include bodies which are not manifestly public authorities, but some of whose functions only are of a public nature. It is relevant to cases where the courts are not sure whether they are looking at a public authority in the full-bloodied [section] 6(1) sense with regard to those bodies which fall into the grey area between public and private. The [Act] reflects the decision to include as 'public authorities' bodies which have some public functions and some private functions.'[1]

---

[1]   HL Committee, 24 November 1997, col 811.

PERMITTED EXCEPTIONS

8.2   Actions of a public authority which are incompatible with a Convention right will not be rendered unlawful in two strict circumstances. First, if as a result of primary legislation the authority *could not have acted differently* (s 6(2)(a)) and secondly, if the authority was *acting to enforce or give effect* to incompatible primary legislation or provisions made under such legislation (s 6(2)(b)) [author's emphasis].

WHAT IS A PUBLIC AUTHORITY?

8.3   A clear definition of the term 'public authority' is absent from the 1998 Act. Instead the Act adopts the use of an interpretative principle to assess whether a body is acting as a public authority for the purposes of the Act (see paras 1.20–1.22 and 8.11, 8.12). Some guidance is provided by way of a broad, inclusive definition. Section 6(3) provides that 'public authority' includes a court or tribunal (s 6(3)(a)) and 'any person certain of whose functions are functions of a public nature' (s 6(3)(b)). It excludes the House of Commons, the House of Lords and 'a person exercising functions in connection with proceedings in Parliament'.

8.4   Courts and tribunals are expressed as public authorities under s 6(3)(a). The House of Lords acting in its judicial capacity is a 'court' will be a public authority for the purposes of s 6. The meaning of 'any person certain of whose functions are functions of a public nature' under s 6(3)(b) is less clear. Does this include, for example, companies and unassociated organisations? Lord Williams of Mostyn, Under-Secretary of State at the Home Office, commented—

> '. . . [Section] 6(3) refers to "any person" . . . the term is well known as a term of art in our law. It is defined in the Interpretation Act 1978 and is relied upon throughout the statute book as including any person or body of persons corporate or unincorporate. I suggest that that is clearly wide enough to cover the natural or legal person . . . '.[1]

---

[1]   HL Committee, 24 November 1997, col 803.

EXCLUSION OF THE HOUSES OF PARLIAMENT

8.5   Speaking on the exclusion of the Houses of Parliament from the ambit of a public authority, the Home Secretary, Jack Straw, stated—

> '[Section] 6 excludes the Houses of Parliament from the category of public authorities for very good reasons. What the Bill makes clear is that Parliament is supreme, and that if Parliament wishes to maintain the position enshrined in an Act that it has passed, but which is incompatible with the Convention in the eyes of a British court, it is that Act which will remain in force.'[1]

---

[1]   HC 2R, 16 February 1998, col 774.

A BROAD DEFINITION OF 'PUBLIC AUTHORITY'

8.6   Much discussion during the parliamentary debates concerned the broad definition under the proposed 1998 Act of a 'public authority'. Several attempts were made to include an exhaustive list of bodies which were capable of being public authorities, but the Government and indeed others such as Lord Lester supported the clause in the form it was later enacted. The most helpful explanation for adopting a broad definition was provided by Lord Lester during the Committee stage of the Bill as it passed through the House of Lords—

'The drafters of the Bill have wisely included a broad, inclusive definition of what constitutes a public authority. They have done so because it is only possible on a case-by-case basis, looking at the particular body, the nature of the functions and the circumstances in which they are discharged, for the courts to come to a conclusion as to whether the activity falls on the side of a public function.

It is not a new problem. Indeed the courts have been seeking to distinguish between those bodies that are subject to the supervisory jurisdiction of the courts in judicial review and those which are not for a number of years. By now, they have developed clear and coherent criteria of a general kind to decide which side of the line a particular body comes within. Therefore, I entirely agree with the need for a broad and inclusive definition rather than some kind of exhaustive list.'[1]

---

[1]   HL Committee, 24 November 1997, col 792.

8.7   Lord Lester helpfully mentions criteria which the court may take into account in assessing a public authority: the nature of the functions of a particular body and the circumstances in which they are discharged. Criteria have already been developed by the High Court in relation to assessing a public authority for the purposes of judicial review proceedings. In Lord Lester's opinion—

'The question to be asked is whether the functions performed by the person concerned are or are not of a public nature. That is exactly the same kind of question as arises all the time under Order 53 of the Rules of the Supreme Court and its counterpart under the Scots rules for judicial review.'[1]

---

[1]   HL Committee, 24 November 1997, col 793.

8.8   All bodies which suspect they might be public authorities for the purposes of s 6 would therefore be well advised to confer with the case law on judicial review proceedings. For, as Lord Williams succinctly stated during Second Reading in the House of Lords—'Every public authority will know that its behaviour, its structures, its conclusions and its executive actions will be subject to this culture.'[2]

---

[1]   HL 2R, 3 November 1997, col 1308.

8.9   Presumably a public authority will 'know', if not before then certainly afterwards, if a case is successfully brought against it by an individual under s 7 which provides victims or potential victims under s 6(1) with the right to bring proceedings against the authority for such acts.[1]

---

[1]   See Ch 9 for commentary on s 7.

THE PRINCIPLE BY WHICH TO ASSESS A PUBLIC AUTHORITY

8.10 Guidance may be taken from the discussions during the Bill's passage through Parliament regarding the principle of a public function by which to assess a public authority. Regarding the criteria in s 6(3) used to determine which bodies may be regarded as public authorities, Lord Irvine explained the following—

> 'There are some bodies which are obviously public authorities such as the police, the courts, government departments and prisons . . . However, [section 6(3)] asks us whether the body in question has certain functions—not all—which are functions of a public nature. If it has any functions of a public nature, it qualifies as a public authority. However, it is certain acts by public authorities which this [Act] makes unlawful. In [section] 6(5) the [Act] provides:
>
> 'In relation to a particular act, a person is not a public authority by virtue only of subsection [(3)] if the nature of the act is private'.
>
> Therefore Railtrack, as a public utility, obviously qualifies as a public authority because some of its functions, for example its functions in relation to safety on the railway, qualify it as a public authority. However, acts carried out in its capacity as a private property developer would no doubt be held by the courts to be of a private nature and therefore not caught by the [Act].'[1]

---

[1]   HL 2R, 3 November 1997, col 796.

8.11 Lord Irvine went on to explain why an exhaustive list of public authorities had not been preferred for inclusion within the Bill—

> '. . . we took a policy decision to avoid a list . . . the disadvantage of a list is precisely the one identified by the noble Lord [Lester] . . . namely, that it would be easy to regard it as exhaustive or to suggest that any non-listed body could be a public authority only if it was sufficiently analogous in its essential characteristics to a body that had qualified in the list. There are obvious public authorities—I have mentioned some—which are covered in relation to the whole of their functions by [section] 6(1). Then there are some bodies some of whose functions are public and some private. If there are some public functions the body qualifies as a public authority but not in respect of acts which are of a private nature. Those statutory principles will have to be applied case by case by the courts when issues arise. We think it is far better to have a principle rather than a list which would be regarded as exhaustive.'[2]

---

[1]   HL 2R, 3 November 1997, col 796.

LIABILITY UNDER s 6

Types of public authority

8.12 There are thus two main types of public authority, first those which are express (courts and tribunals: s 6(3)(a)) or 'obvious' public authorities (such as the police, government departments and immigration officials: see para 8.10), which will be liable under s 6 for all their actions, regardless of the public or private nature of the acts in question. The other category consists of those bodies which fall into the 'grey' area and which exercise both public and private functions. These bodies will only be liable under s 6 for acts performed in the exercise of their 'public functions'. Actions by such quasi-public authorities which are of a private nature will not attract liability under s 6, as provided by s 6(5).

8.13 Members from both Houses of Parliament during debates on the Bill attempted to obtain from the Government examples of the types of bodies which may fall within the scope of a 'public authority'. Whilst the Government always gave deference to the assessment of a public authority being 'a matter for the courts', it gave some examples as follows—

General

'[a] question about the definition of a public authority. Does a body that spends taxpayers' money, or fulfils a statutory function, or has Government appointees on its governing body constitute a public authority for the purposes of the Bill?'

Mike O'Brien, Parliamentary Under-Secretary of State for the Home Department—'That will be a matter for the courts, but it would appear likely to be so.'[1]

Television companies

'[It] is ultimately a matter for the courts, but our judgment is that the BBC will be regarded as a public authority under [section] 6; independent companies will not, but the Independent Television Commission will be.'[2]

Newspapers

'My Lords, subject to the cautious proviso that this is a matter for the courts to determine in due time, it is our belief that a newspaper is not a public authority . . .'[3]

Charities

' . . . charities that operate, let us say, in the area of homelessness, no doubt do exercise public functions. The NSPCC, for example, exercises statutory functions which are of a public nature, although it is a charity.'[4]

Prosecuting authorities

'As a matter of principle it is plain that a prosecuting authority is a public authority and that it is right that it should abstain from acting in a way which is incompatible with one or more of the Convention rights, but if it does so act, then it acts unlawfully.'[5]

Private security companies

'A private security company would be exercising public functions in relation to the management of a contracted-out prison but would be acting privately when, for example, guarding commercial premises.'[6]

Doctors

> 'Doctors in general practice would be public authorities in relation to their National Health Service functions, but not in relation to their private patients.'[7]

---

[1]   Sir Brian Mawhinney: HC 2R, 16 February 1998, col 860.
[2]   Jack Straw: HC 2R, 16 February 1998, col 778.
[3]   Lord Williams: HL 2R, 3 November 1997, col 1310. For more detail on the effects of the Act on the press, see commentary on s 12 at Ch 14.
[4]   Lord Irvine of Lairg: HL Committee, 24 November 1997, col 800.
[5]   Ibid, col 808.
[6]   Ibid, col 811.
[7]   Ibid, col 811.

Privatised industries

8.14   Many privatised industries carry out functions that were once performed by public authorities, and are thus susceptible to liability for such acts under the jurisdiction of the High Court in judicial review proceedings and before the European Court of Human Rights. For these reasons it is likely that privatised industries will fall within the scope of s 6, at least so far as their 'public' functions are concerned.

8.15   As Jack Straw explained—

> 'The Bill had to have a definition of public authority that went at least as wide and took account of the fact that, over the past 20 years, an increasingly large number of private bodies, such as companies or charities, have come to exercise public functions that were previously exercised by public authorities. Under UK domestic common law, such bodies have increasingly been held to account under the process of judicial review.'[1]

---

[1]   HC 2R, 16 February 1998, col 775.

8.16   On the matter of international responsibility for acts by privatised bodies, Lord Lester commented—

> ' . . . refer[ring] to the problem of privatised industries. It is clear from the case law of the European Court of Human Rights that, where a body that is private in form is performing a function that would otherwise be performed by a public authority, there would be international liability if that body did not comply properly with the Convention. Perhaps we can imagine, for example, the privatisation of the Prison Service. It would be unthinkable if a body which was private in form but public in function could escape liability under the Convention.'[1]

---

[1]   HL Committee, 24 November 1997, col 792.

Acts and omissions of public authorities

8.17   Section 6(1) states that it is unlawful for a public authority to *act* in a way which is incompatible with a Convention right [author's emphasis]. Section 6(6) clarifies the meaning of 'an act' as including a failure to act. Mike O'Brien explained that unintentional failures to act might also be caught by the section—

'. . . As for omissions, the [Act] . . . provides, in [section] 6, that an act includes a failure to act. This goes wider than deliberate failures: an unintentional failure to act by a public authority is to be open to challenge under the [Act] in the same way as any other failure to act, if that failure is incompatible with Convention rights . . . our courts are familiar with on-going omissions and are able to deal with them in the appropriate way.'[1]

---

[1]   HC Committee, 24 June 1998, col 1097.

IMMUNITY UNDER s 6

Excluded omissions

8.18   Specifically excluded from liability for failure to act is the failure 'to introduce in, or lay before, Parliament a proposal for legislation' (s 6(6)(a)) or a failure to 'make any primary legislation or remedial order' (s 6(6)(b)). This is in accordance with s 6(3) by which Parliament is not a public authority for the purposes of s 6. Thus any risk arising from the application of s 6 to the sovereignty of Parliament to legislate is abrogated, and Ministers who decline to use their powers to initiate remedial action and orders under HRA 1998, s 10 and Sch 2 following the making of declaration of incompatibility are exempted from liability.

Private individuals

8.19   It is Parliament's intention that s 6 should not apply to private individuals. The Government's approach to the application of HRA 1998 to public authorities was clearly explained by Lord Irvine during Second Reading of the Bill by the House of Lords—

'. . . about our approach to the application of this [Act] to public authorities . . . We decided . . . that a provision of this kind should apply only to public authorities, however defined, and not to private individuals. That reflects the arrangements for taking cases to the Convention institutions in Strasbourg. The Convention had its origins in a desire to protect people from the misuse of power by the State, rather than from the actions of private individuals. Someone who takes a case to Strasbourg is proceeding against the United Kingdom Government, rather than against a private individual. We also decided that we should apply the [Act] to a wide rather than a narrow range of public authorities, so as to provide as much protection as possible to those who claim that their rights have been infringed.

[Section] 6 is designed to apply not only to obvious public authorities such as government departments and the police, but also to bodies which are public in certain respects but not others. Organisations of this kind will be liable under [section] 6 of the [Act] for any of their acts, unless the act is of a private nature. Finally, [section] 6 does not impose a liability on organisations which have no public functions at all.'[1]

---

[1]   HL 2R, 3 November 1997, col 1231.

---

9 Proceedings

CONVENTION RIGHTS IN LEGAL PROCEEDINGS

9.1 The Home Secretary, Jack Straw, described the purpose of s 7 as follows—

'[Section] 7 enables individuals who believe that they have been a victim of an unlawful act of a public authority to rely on the Convention rights in legal proceedings. They may do so in a number of ways: by bringing proceedings under the [Act] in an appropriate court or tribunal; in seeking judicial review; as part of a defence against criminal or civil action brought against them by a public authority; or in the course of an appeal. [Section] 7 ensures that an individual will always have a means by which to raise his or her Convention rights. It is intended that existing court procedures will, wherever possible, be used for that purpose.'[1]

---

[1] HC 2R, 16 February 1998, col 780.

9.2 The effect of s 7 is to permit individuals for the first time to apply directly to a domestic court or tribunal for the determination of alleged breaches of their Convention rights. Prior to the 1998 Act an individual's only recourse for such a determination was to apply to Strasbourg. Section 7 thus creates a new cause of action in legal proceedings where it is alleged that a public authority acted unlawfully under s 6 of the 1998 Act, based upon respect for the rights and freedoms termed within the Act as 'the Convention rights' (see para 1.6).

9.3 However, as discussed below, the accessibility of the new cause of action provided by s 7 is dependent upon an individual passing a new test of standing for domestic proceedings, namely that he or she be a 'victim' of the unlawful act in question.

RAISING A CONVENTION ARGUMENT BEFORE THE DOMESTIC COURTS

9.4 A person who is a victim or a potential victim of the unlawful act may—
— bring proceedings against the authority under the Act in the appropriate court or tribunal (s 7(1)(a)),
— rely on the Convention rights concerned in any legal proceedings (s 7(1)(b)).

Bringing a case under HRA 1998

9.5 Section 7(1)(a) states that a person may bring proceedings for breach of their Convention rights, including a counterclaim or similar action (s 7(2)), against a public authority in the 'appropriate court or tribunal'. This provides a new, free-standing cause of action against a public authority for acting in a manner which is incompatible with the Convention rights. In the Government's view claims under s 7(1)(a) will be rare, and it was felt undesirable to exclude tribunals from hearing such claims—'we expect that such cases will be relatively infrequent, but where they do arise, it is likely that a tribunal will sometimes be the most appropriate forum for hearing the case.'[1]

---

[1] Mike O'Brien, Parliamentary Under-Secretary of State for the Home Department: HC Committee, 24 June 1998, col 1056.

Appropriate courts and tribunals

9.6   An 'appropriate court or tribunal' is to be determined in accordance with 'rules' (s 7(2)), to be made under the powers contained within s 7(9). These rules will be exercised by the Lord Chancellor, the Secretary of State or a Northern Ireland department, depending upon whether the proceedings are held in a court or tribunal outside Scotland (s 7(9)(a)), within Scotland (s 7(9)(b)) or before a tribunal in Northern Ireland (s 7(9)(c)). In making such rules, regard must be had by the Minister or department to s 9, which applies to s 7(1)(a) proceedings brought in respect of a judicial act (s 7(10)).[1] The rules on appropriate courts and tribunals had not been drafted at the time this book went to print.

---

[1] See further commentary to s 9 at Ch 11.

Limitation period

9.7   Section 7(5) provides a limitation period for cases brought under s 7(1)(a). Such proceedings must be brought 'before the end of the period of one year beginning with the date on which the act complained of took place' (s 7(5)(a)), or 'such longer period as the court or tribunal considers equitable having regard to all the circumstances' (s 7(5)(b)). The limitation period provided by s 7(5) is expressly subject to 'any rule imposing a stricter time limit in relation to the procedure in question'. For example, the shorter time limit in relation to judicial review proceedings will continue to apply (ie the application should be made promptly and in any event within three months of the action complained of).[1]

---

[1] Mike O'Brien: 'Assuming that the new rules of court that will be needed for the [Act] provide that a procedure analogous to judicial review may be used for cases under [section] 7(1)(a), it is reasonable that the time limit for that procedure—which is three months—should continue to apply. It would not be right for applicants who choose to bring their claims by way of judicial review to benefit from the longer 12-month period proposed for claims under the [Act].' HC Committee, 24 June 1998, col 1094.

9.8   A desire to impose a limitation period for s 7(1)(a) actions to be brought emerged during consideration of the Bill in Committee by the House of Commons. There was consensus between the parties on the need for a limitation period, although there was variation in the time limits suggested. The Government's proposal of a limitation period of one year was finally accepted by 232 votes to 34.[1] Mike O'Brien explained the rationale behind the limitation period proposed (successfully) by the Government's amendment—

> '[T]here is at present a range of limitations periods in our law. For judicial review proceedings, an application for leave must be made

promptly and in any event within three months; for cases of personal injury caused by negligence, it is three years; and for most other actions in tort, it is six years . . . What we have tried to do in our amendment is to strike a balance between the legitimate needs of the plaintiff and the legitimate needs of the defendant, which is what all limitation periods should do.

Proceedings under [section] 7(1)(a) will always be against a public authority, alleging that it has acted in a way that is incompatible with a Convention right. Not all the public authorities concerned will be government authorities in the narrow sense . . . The authority and those who are affected by its decisions are entitled to expect that proceedings of a novel character, if they are to be brought at all, will be brought promptly.'[2]

---

[1]   HC Committee, 24 June 1998, col 1102. Edward Garnier (Harborough) had earlier moved and then, following debate, withdrawn, an amendment to include a three month time limit for all claims under s 7(1)(a); see further ibid, cols 1091–1100.

[2]   HC Committee, 24 June 1998, col 1095.

9.9   On the inclusion of the court's discretion to extend time for s 7(1)(a) claims when it is considered 'equitable' to do so under s 7(5)(b), Mike O'Brien continued—

'We recognise, however, that there may be circumstances where a rigid one-year cut off could lead to injustice. Our amendment does not therefore seek to provide a rigid limit, but enables the court to extend the period where it is appropriate to do so. There will be cases in which an individual has good reason for delay. In judicial review cases, for example, the courts have extended time where the applicant has been seeking redress by other proper means, such as by pursuing internal grievance procedures, or where he has had to apply for legal aid. I have no doubt that the courts will continue to exercise their discretion so as to prevent prejudice to one party or the other where an application is made to extend time.'[1]

---

[1]   HC Committee, 24 June 1998, col 1096.

9.10 The courts are well-versed in applying equitable standards to extend time limits where permitted to do so under statute, and will not be placed in difficulties in applying s 7(5)(b). For example, limitation periods which apply to proceedings brought under the Sex Discrimination Act 1975 have been regularly extended by employment tribunals where they have found 'just and equitable' grounds to do so—'just and equitable' being the criteria required to justify a time extension under the 1975 Act. Similarly, as the courts begin to apply HRA 1998 a body of case law will undoubtedly emerge concerning situations where the courts deem it 'equitable' to extend the limitation period provided therein.

Reliance on the Convention rights in any legal proceedings

9.11 Section 7(1)(b) provides that a person who claims that a public authority has acted unlawfully under s 6(1), or proposes to so act, may rely on the Convention right(s) in any legal proceedings. Under s 7(6) the term 'legal proceedings' includes[1] proceedings brought by or at the instigation of a public authority (s 7(6)(a)) and an appeal against the decision of a court or tribunal (s 7(6)(b)). The use of the term 'any legal proceedings' means that under s 7(1)(b) an individual is not required to initiate proceedings directly under HRA 1998 against a public authority in order to enforce his Convention right(s). A person may cite their Convention right(s) in any legal proceedings to which he and the public authority are parties. Examples of this might be as a defence in criminal proceedings in a magistrates' court (where both the Crown Prosecution Service and the court are public authorities), or as a counterclaim to a possession action brought by a county council in the county court or as one of the grounds of appeal before an immigration adjudicator, or as a ground of appeal against any decision taken by a lower court. (See para 19.12 as to retrospective application of HRA 1998 to s 7(1)(b) claims.

---

[1] ' . . . [section] 7(5) uses the word 'includes' and is therefore not . . . an exhaustive definition': Mike O'Brien, HC Committee, 24 June 1998, col 1057.

The prevalence of s 7(1)(b) claims

9.12 Mike O'Brien stated that the Government anticipated that most Convention arguments would fall within the second limb of s 7, namely s 7(1)(b), and that it was important to allow such claims to be brought before tribunals in addition to the courts—

> 'It is our expectation that the great majority of cases in which the Convention arguments are raised will fall within the scope of such proceedings. That is because, in most cases, it is likely that a victim of an act made unlawful by [section] 6(1) will have available to him an existing course of action or other means of legal challenge, such as a judicial review.
>
> Furthermore, in a significant proportion of such cases, a tribunal, not a court, will be the forum in which a case is brought. Social security, employment, housing and immigration are but a few of the many areas where tribunals handle the bulk of cases . . . to prevent individuals from raising Convention points in tribunals would cause unnecessary delay, expense and frustration.'[1]

---

[1] HC Committee, 24 June 1998, col 1056.

Relevance of HRA 1998 in proceedings between private individuals

9.13 Edward Garnier (Conservative) questioned whether the proceedings referred to in s 7(5) included prosecutions other than those brought, for example, by the Crown Prosecution Service or Her Majesty's Customs and Excise. He asked the Government—

> ' . . . would Marks and Spencer, Tesco, Sainsbury or any shopkeeper who wanted to bring a private prosecution for shoplifting be deemed to be a public authority under the definition in [section] 6, for the purposes of [section] 7(5) and the instigation of proceedings?'[1]

Mike O'Brien replied—

> 'The vast majority of criminal proceedings will be caught directly by [section] 7(5)(a) as they are
>
> 'proceedings brought by or at the instigation of a public authority'.

The very few private prosecutions that are undertaken will also be caught by [section] 7(5)—as it is an inclusive definition, and such prosecutions would be regarded as legal proceedings. In such cases, the private prosecutor would not be a public authority, although the court, as a public authority, would be required to act not incompatibly with the Convention rights. Therefore, Tesco, for example, would not become a public authority. *The court itself will be required to take account of the Convention rights'* [author's emphasis].[2]

---

[1]   HC Committee, 24 June 1998, col 1055.

[2]   Ibid, col 1057.

9.14 This statement illustrates the effect that HRA 1998 may have on proceedings between private individuals. It follows that a court, as a public authority under s 6, is required, in all cases before it, to 'take account of the Convention rights', regardless of whether the parties to the proceedings includes a public authority or not.

LOCUS STANDI: THE VICTIM TEST

9.15 The right to rely on s 7 in the domestic courts is restricted to a person who is (or would be) a victim of the unlawful act (s 7(7)). Section 7(7) explains that 'for the purposes of this section, a person is a victim of an unlawful act only if he would be a victim for the purposes of Art 34 of the Convention if proceedings were brought in the European Court of Human Rights in respect of that act.'

Section 7 and Art 34 of the Convention

9.16 Prior to the entering into force of Protocol 11 to the European Convention on Human Rights on 1 November 1998, applications by citizens of the States Parties alleging violations of their Convention rights by their Governments fell to the competence of the Commission under Art 25 of the Convention. Only those applications which fulfilled the admissibility requirements and which met the 'victim' requirement could ultimately be referred on to the Court. Article 34 of the Convention is the successor to Art 25 and recognises that the Court of Human Rights is now the organ to which all such applications should be directed—

'The Court may receive applications from any person, non-governmental organisation or group of individuals claiming to be the victim of a violation by one of the High Contracting Parties of the rights set forth in the Convention or the protocols thereto. The High Contracting Parties undertake not to hinder in any way the effective exercise of this right'.

9.17 Article 34, as with many of the Convention provisions, provides broad propositions. The concept of what constitutes a 'victim' has been defined by case law emanating from the Commission and Court, although the decisions of the two organs have not always tallied. The corpus of jurisprudence on this issue is complex and unresolved issues remain. At present there is no case which has been considered in Strasbourg that offers a comprehensive analysis of the victim requirement.

However, standing, under s 7 of the Act, reflects standing under Art 34, and as such it is essential for legal practitioners to familiarise themselves with the Strasbourg jurisprudence in this area.

9.18 The 'victim test' is a new test insofar as proceedings before the UK courts are concerned. The victim test under Art 34 of the Convention requires a person seeking to plead Convention rights to have been directly affected, or to be potentially directly affected, by the allegedly unlawful act by the public authority in question. Such a rule of standing is novel insofar as application by domestic courts are concerned, although in private law proceedings before the domestic courts, for example claims for damages in tort or breach of statutory duty, claimants have to show they were personally affected by the breach of duty alleged, a test which is not so far removed from the victim requirement.

The victim test in judicial review proceedings

9.19 In public law proceedings, however, such as judicial review, the onus is not on the rights of the private individual or corporation, but on the exercise of powers and discretions of a public body. Accordingly, standing for judicial review is based on a party proving 'sufficient interest' in the matter to which the application relates. The British courts have interpreted this to include applications for judicial review by representative groups and public interest groups. Under the new victim requirement, however, such groups will be debarred from bringing judicial review applications based on Convention rights in their own name, unless the group can show that it is 'directly' affected. Instead, such a group may support applications by individuals under HRA 1998. The consequence of this movement from the established domestic test of 'sufficient interest' to the new victim test is that whereas the courts have been able in the past to consider the wider public interest in cases brought by representative groups, and to rule accordingly, under HRA 1998 the courts may only consider the effect on the individual concerned, although groups of individuals may claim redress if they are all 'victims'.

9.20 Section 7(3) and (4) relate specifically to proceedings for unlawful acts brought against public authorities by way of judicial review in England, Wales and in Scotland. For a person to have 'sufficient interest' in England and Wales or to have 'title and interest to sue' in Scotland, ie the respective tests of standing for judicial review applications or petitions, the 1998 Act requires the person bringing the judicial review proceedings to be a victim or potential victim of the unlawful act by a public authority.

9.21 The effects of importing the concept of the victim test will be far-reaching for several reasons. For the courts, the victim requirement represents a departure from normal British rules governing standing in administrative law cases and from the tried and tested case law of what amounts to sufficient interest in judicial review proceedings. Most notably, whilst public interest groups have been held to possess sufficient interest before the High Court and have been permitted to mount challenges against public bodies, under the Strasbourg test, such groups are not 'victims'. The courts will have to have regard to the complex body of Strasbourg case law on the concept of 'victim', which unfortunately does not provide as much clarity as the domestic case law on judicial review. Finally, individuals will also have to seek guidance on the Strasbourg 'victim' test if they are ever to mount a successful action under s 7. Failure to do so may result in such an action falling at the first hurdle of standing.

9.22 Section 7(8) provides that nothing in HRA 1998 creates a criminal offence.

9.23 Rules may be made by the relevant Minister, under s 7(9), to determine which courts and tribunals are to be empowered to hear s 7 proceedings (as to rules made under s 7(9) see para 19.2). Further, under s 7(11), the relevant Minister may extend the relief or remedies granted by a court or tribunal or the grounds on which it may grant any of them. Section 7(11) was specifically drafted to include within the powers of immigration tribunals and special adjudicators the power to consider Convention rights issues and the power to grant relief in respect of successful actions (see further para 19.4).[1]

---

1   Mike O'Brien: 'The power conferred by [section 7(11)] has been included to cater for situations where the grounds on which proceedings may be brought before a tribunal are extremely narrowly defined either by statute or by restrictive judicial interpretation of statutory provisions. In those rare cases, a tribunal would, unless its powers were suitably amplified, be precluded from determining issues relating to the convention rights. The issue that prompted the inclusion of [section 7(11)] is the constraints placed on special adjudicators hearing appeals under the Asylum and Immigration Tribunals Act 1993.
. . . the terms of the 1993 Act are such that they would prevent a special adjudicator hearing an asylum case from determining whether an appellant's removal from the United Kingdom would breach his convention rights when such appeals were dealt with.' HC Committee, 24 June 1998, col 1109.

10 Judicial remedies

REMEDIAL SCOPE OF s 8

10.1 The Lord Chancellor, Lord Irvine of Lairg, explained the remedial scope of s 8 as follows—

> 'If a court or tribunal finds that a public authority has acted in a way which is incompatible with the Convention, what can it do about it? Under [section] 8 it may provide whatever remedy is available to it and which seems just and appropriate. That might include awarding damages against the public authority. We have concluded that if a court is considering an award of damages for an act which is incompatible with the Convention, then it should have regard to the principles applied by the European Court of Human Rights. Our aim is that people should receive damages equivalent to what they would have obtained had they taken their case to Strasbourg.'[1]

---

[1]   HL 2R, 3 November 1997, col 1232.

10.2 Section 8(1) provides that where a court (or tribunal s 8(6)) finds an act or a proposed act of a public authority to be unlawful, it may 'grant such relief or remedy, or make such order, within its powers as it considers just and appropriate'. The phrase 'within its powers' restricts the power of the courts to grant any new remedies, as set out in s 8(2) which provides that '. . . damages may be awarded only by a court which has power to award damages, or to order the payment of compensation, in civil proceedings'. However, the phrase 'within its powers' also authorises the courts to make use of the best remedies they have at their disposal under the common law.

THE CORRECT FORUM TO PURSUE AN AWARD OF DAMAGES

10.3 Pursuant to s 8(2) criminal courts, for example, which do not have the power to award damages in civil proceedings, may not award damages to a defendant whose Convention rights are found by the court to have been infringed by a public authority. This is so even where a criminal court has the power to award compensation in criminal proceedings, but not in civil proceedings, for example a magistrates' court. Instead, the individual concerned will have to pursue damages for the breach in the civil courts, which have such a power.

10.4 The criminal courts may, however, grant any remedy which they already have the power to grant in criminal proceedings upon finding there has been a s 6(1) unlawful act, such as quashing a conviction, foreseen as a likely remedy by the White Paper— 'In some cases, the right course may be for the decision of the public authority to be quashed.'[1] The reason for restricting criminal courts from granting damages in criminal cases under the 1998 Act was explained by Lord Irvine during consideration of the Bill in Committee—

'[Section 8 provides] a comprehensive and comprehensible code. However, it is necessary to put down certain limits on what remedies a court or tribunal can provide. Subsection (2) . . . provides one such restriction. It states that,

'damages may be awarded only by a court which has power to award damages . . . in civil proceedings.'

Quite clearly, this means that a criminal court will not be able to award damages for a Convention breach, even if it currently has the power to make a compensation order unless it also has the power to award damages in civil proceedings.

So as to make the intention plain, it is not the [Act's] aim that, for example, the Crown court should be able to make an award of damages where it finds, during the course of a trial, that a violation of a person's Convention rights has occurred. We believe that it is appropriate for an individual who considers that his rights have been infringed in such a case to pursue any matter of damages through the civil courts where this type of issue is normally dealt with; in other words, to pursue the matter in the courts that are accustomed to determining whether it is necessary and appropriate to award damages and what the proper amount should be. For that reason, we regard the inclusion of subsection (2) as an entirely proper part of the scheme.

We say that the Crown Court, in cases of crime, should not award damages. The remedy that the defendant wants in a criminal court is not to be convicted. We see very practical difficulties about giving a new power to award damages to a criminal court in Convention cases . . . We believe [it] would be potentially disruptive of a criminal trial. Similarly, a magistrates' court is a criminal court . . . We believe that it is appropriate that the civil courts, which traditionally make awards of damages, should, alone, be enabled to make awards of damages in these Convention cases.'[2]

---

[1]   'Rights Brought Home: The Human Rights Bill', Cm 3782 (1997), para 2.10.
[2]   HL Committee, 24 November 1997, col 854.

THE CRITERIA FOR GRANTING AN AWARD OF DAMAGES

10.5 Section 8(3) provides in strict terms that 'No award of damages is to be made unless, taking account of all the circumstances of the case . . . the court is satisfied that the award is necessary to afford just satisfaction to the person in whose favour it is made'. This provision demonstrates that the intention of Parliament is not for the courts to provide damages in each and every case where a violation of the Convention rights is found to have occurred. While taking account of all the circumstances of the case a court should have regard to two specific factors in determining an award of damages, namely any other remedy, relief or order granted by any court in relation to the unlawful act in question (s 8(3)(a)) and the consequences of any decision of any court in respect of that act (s 8(3)(b)). It is clear therefore that an award of damages is only to be regarded as a last remedial resort.

10.6 The reference to 'just satisfaction' in s 8(3) is taken from the wording of Art 41 of the Convention, which is expressly mentioned in s 8(4) (see para 10.8). Article 41 provides—

> 'If the Court finds there has been a violation of the Convention or the protocols thereto, *and if the internal law of the High Contracting Party concerned allows only partial reparation to be made,* the Court shall, if necessary afford just satisfaction to the injured party.' [author's emphasis].

10.7 When considering the wording of Art 41 and the wording of s 8(3) together, it is clear that the direction to the courts in s 8(3)(a) and (b) attempts to mirror the provisions of Art 41. It is likely that only in the event of a domestic court finding that no reparation or only partial reparation has been provided to the individual concerned for the unlawful act might a court then venture into considering whether to award damages as 'just satisfaction'. This reasoning is similar to the grant of an injunction by a domestic court; if damages are an appropriate remedy the injunction will not be granted. Under HRA 1998, s 8, damages will only be granted where there is no other appropriate remedy.

10.8 Section 8(4) directs the court, in determining whether to award damages (s 8(4)(a)) or the amount of the award (s 8(4)(b)), to take into account the principles applied by the Strasbourg Court in relation to the award of compensation under Art 41 of the Convention. As Lord Irvine pointed out, the direction in s 8(4) that the courts 'must take into account' the Strasbourg Court's principles bears the same meaning as the use of the phrase 'must take into account' under s 2 of the Act—

> '... in [section] 8, the wording of subsection (4) is consistent with that used in [section] 2; namely, that in determining whether to award damages, or the amount of an award, a court "must take into account" the principles applied by the European Court of Human Rights in relation to the award of compensation ... the similar expressions in two parts of the [Act] will bear the same meaning. The intention of [section] 8 is that people should, so far as is possible, receive the same remedies from our domestic courts—albeit with much less delay—as they would receive if the case went to Strasbourg. For that to happen, it is necessary that our courts should take into account the principles adopted by the European Court of Human Rights ... the phrase, "take into account", allows the courts to use their discretion where appropriate in applying Strasbourg jurisprudence generally to cases before them. It would be unnecessary and confusing to have a different phrase in [section] 8 from that in [section] 2. It would suggest that the courts were to apply a different test in questions of damages, which is contrary to our intentions.'[1]

---

[1] HL Report, 29 January 1998, col 387.

A PRINCIPLED APPROACH TO THE AWARD OF DAMAGES?

10.9 The reference to the phrase 'principles applied by the European Court of Human Rights in relation to the award of compensation' is ambiguous since in the rare event of the court awarding damages as 'just satisfaction' the reasoning is limited to the facts of an individual case. There is no common thread which passes through the Convention case law in this regard and which provides a principled approach relating to situations where damages may be appropriate as just satisfaction. The use of the word 'principles' in s 8(4) of the Act is rather misleading, and could undoubtedly cause inexperienced lawyers to attempt to unravel the complex Strasbourg decisions on the award of damages as just satisfaction to find a non-existent principle.[1] In many cases the Court has found that a finding of a violation itself amounts to 'just satisfaction' and that no further recompense is appropriate. In other cases, however, the Court has deemed it appropriate to grant damages of a pecuniary (quantifiable financial loss, eg income) and non-pecuniary (emotional distress, pain and suffering) nature and costs.[2]

---

[1]   For example, the Explanatory and Financial Memorandum to the Human Rights Bill stated 'the awards at Strasbourg "tend to range from £5000 to £15,000 and are not made simply because the Court finds a violation of the Convention . . . "'.

[2]   See paras 1.28–1.34.

10.10   Mike O'Brien, Parliamentary Under-Secretary of State for the Home Department, attempted to shed light on the Court's practice in awarding compensation under Art 41 of the Convention—

> 'It may help if I say something about the principles applied by the European Court of Human Rights in relation to the award of compensation. [Article 41 of the Convention] . . . provides that in the event of a finding of a violation,

> 'the decision of the Court shall, if necessary, afford just satisfaction to the injured party.'

> There is no entitlement to an award, and the court's discretion is guided by the particular circumstances of each and every case. On many occasions, the court has held that no award should be made because the finding of a violation itself constituted just satisfaction. It appears from the court's judgments that matters such as the applicant's conduct and the limited nature of the breach are relevant factors.'[1]

---

[1]   HC Committee, 24 June 1998, col 1114.

AWARD OF DAMAGES: CONTRIBUTION BETWEEN THE PARTIES

10.11   Section 8(5) empowers the court to order contribution towards damages where more than one public authority is held to be responsible for the s 6(1) unlawful act. Mike O'Brien, speaking during Committee, explained why the Government felt it necessary to include a reference to the Civil Liability (Contribution) Act 1978 and the equivalent Scottish legislation—

> 'The Civil Liability (Contribution) Act 1978 provides a right to contribution when more than one person is liable for the same damage. We see no reason why that standard provision should not apply when damages are awarded against a public authority under [section] 8 of the Bill. The amendment makes it clear that the terms of the 1978 Act and

the relevant provisions in Scotland—section 3 of the Law Reform (Miscellaneous Provisions) (Scotland) Act 1940—apply to the award of such damages.'[1]

---

[1]   HC Committee, 24 June 1998, col 1113.

THE INTERRELATION BETWEEN ART 13 AND HRA 1998, s 8

10.12   Article 13 states the following—

'Everyone whose rights and freedoms as set forth in this Convention are violated shall have an effective remedy before a national authority notwithstanding that the violation has been committed by persons acting in an official capacity'.

As mentioned in the commentary to s 1 (at paras 3.13–3.18) the Government justified omitting Art 13 from the list of 'the Convention rights' under s 1(1) of the 1998 Act by stating that 'our view is, quite unambiguously, that Article 13 is met by the passage of the Bill'.[1] HRA 1998, s 8 provides individuals with the novel right to a remedy before the domestic courts where a public authority has acted in breach of the Convention rights (see Ch 12 on remedies). The question arises as to the effectiveness of the remedies provided by the 1998 Act and whether it satisfies the requirements of Art 13.

---

[1]   Lord Williams of Mostyn, Under-Secretary of State at the Home Office: HL 2R, 3 November 1997, col 1308.

10.13   In the opinion of Lord Irvine—

'At present, I cannot conceive of any state of affairs in which an English court, having held an Act to be unlawful because of its infringement of a Convention right, would under [section] 8(1), be disabled from giving an effective remedy. I believe that the English law is rich in remedies and I cannot conceive of a case in which English law under [section] 8(1) would be unable to provide an effective remedy.'[1]

---

[1]   HL Committee, 18 November 1997, col 479.

10.14   If the courts already have the ability to provide effective remedies for breaches of the Convention rights in every case, why not simply include Art 13 in the list of Convention rights enumerated in s 1(1)? Lord Irvine commented—

'The courts would be bound to ask themselves what was intended beyond the existing scheme of remedies set out in the [Act]. It might lead them to fashion remedies other than the [section] 8 remedies, which we regard as sufficient and clear.'[1]

---

[1]   HL Committee, 18 November 1997, col 475.

Judicial innovation under the common law?

10.15   The intention of Parliament regarding the powers of the courts to grant remedies for breach of HRA 1998 is clear, ie judicial innovation, insofar as the provision of remedies are concerned, is to be restrained in accordance with the courts' existing powers. While courts may be formally restrained by statute concerning the remedies they may grant, the question concerning the powers to grant remedies under the common law needs to be addressed.

10.16   Lord Irvine felt that judges ought not be constrained by their purposive approach in the development of the common law under the 1998 Act when he said—'It must be emphasised that the judges are free to develop the common law in their own independent judicial sphere'.[1] This may explain why, under HRA 1998, s 3, it is legislation only which is to be read in light of Strasbourg case law on the Convention Rights. It is arguable that it is implicit that the development of the common law in line with the Convention is a matter to be entrusted to the judges. Compatible common law may be developed in line with the Convention as a whole, and not simply in respect of those 'Convention rights' enumerated in s 1(1). There is no bar to the common law developing in this way, particularly since it is excluded from the injunction in s 3(2) that incompatible statute law remains in force. The role of developing the common law is a matter for the judges, as distinct from the role of creating legislation which is a matter solely for Parliament. The common law may thus be as adaptable as ever, as long as it does not limit the Convention rights protected by HRA 1998, s 1(1). It may also be that the common law might recognise the Convention in a more absolute way than the courts are permitted to under the Act, in considering the Convention as a whole and not simply those rights which are enumerated in s 1(1).

---

[1]   HL Committee, 24 November 1997, col 784.

10.17   Section 7(1)(b) permits Convention arguments to be raised in any legal proceedings to which the public authority is a party and means that the courts will inevitably have to apply the Convention to the common law just as they are directed to apply the Convention to statute law under s 3. Ultimately, it remains to be seen just how proactive a role the judges play in developing the common law and its remedies in line with the Convention. Undoubtedly however, the Act presents the courts with an interpretative challenge, which most judges will relish.

10.18   Lord Irvine made it clear, however, particularly with regard to the Convention right to privacy, that the courts are not permitted under the 1998 Act to act as legislators and to make new law in order to protect a Convention right when they find that neither the common law nor statute protect it, unless the common law so provides—

> 'In my opinion, the court is not obliged to remedy the failure by legislating via the common law either where a Convention right is infringed by incompatible legislation or where, because of the absence of legislation—say, privacy legislation—a Convention right is left unprotected. In my view, the courts may not act as legislators and grant

new remedies for infringement of Convention rights *unless the common law itself enables them to develop new rights or remedies'* [author's emphasis].[1]

---

[1]   HL Committee, 24 November 1997, col 785.

EFFECTIVE REMEDIES

10.19   During the Report stage of the Bill in the House of Lords, Lord Irvine expressed his satisfaction at the scope of remedies available under s 8 notwithstanding the omission from HRA 1998 of Art 13 of the Convention—

> 'Our courts are rich in remedies and have every freedom under [section] 8.
>
> . . . The [Act] has been constructed in a way that affords ample protection for individuals' rights under the Convention. We have adopted an intentionally wide definition of public authority under [section] 6, and [section] 8(1) . . . gives the courts ample scope for doing justice when unlawful acts are committed.
>
> . . . I have not the least idea what the remedies the courts might develop outside [section] 8 could be if Article 13 was included . . . [section] 8(1) is of the widest amplitude. No one is contending that it will not do the job. When we have challenged the proponents of the amendment on a number of a occasions in Committee to say how [section] 8 might not do the job, they have been unable to offer a single example . . . What we have done is sufficient.'[1]

---

[1]   HL Report, 19 January 1998, col 1266.

Exceptions

10.20   Are there any instances where the courts might not be entitled to provide an effective remedy? Lord Lester, during Committee in the House of Lords, questioned whether the Act permits a court, for example in judicial review proceedings, to grant compensation as a remedy for a public law wrongdoing. He pointed out that English law currently only allows compensation as a remedy in public law where there has been a misfeasance in public office. It is common practice for the courts to grant compensation in relation to private law torts. It is questionable however whether the courts can grant compensation for public law torts under the Act—

> ' . . . one cannot obtain compensation under traditional English legal principles for maladministration unless there is misfeasance in the public office, unless there is bad faith. However under the European Convention on Human Rights, the position is somewhat different.
>
> It is clear that where a public authority acts in breach of legitimate expectations in a public law context and causes direct damage, there is a right under the Convention to compensation. What I am not clear about as regards the structure of [section] 8 as it stands is what happens in, for example, judicial review proceedings, where what is at stake is a

public law tort (a government tort) giving rise to direct loss, as distinct from the normal private law tort. The distinction does not usually arise under our legal system as it stands, except, as I say, where there is a misfeasance in public office.

If I am right about the position under the European Convention—it arises in the Irish case called *Pine Valley Developments*, where the European Court held that there needed to be compensation for breach of legitimate expectations in the planning context—it seems to me that one needs to be clear whether, by means of a *Pepper v Hart* statement, or under the wording of [section] 8, the [Act] permits the remedy of compensation for what I call public law wrongdoing as distinct from normal private law tort in the context in which the Convention would require it.'[1]

---

[1]   HL Committee, 24 November 1997, col 854.

10.21   The answer remains to be seen, as Lord Irvine provided no guidance to Lord Lester's question. Arguably, it might take some development of the common law first. The restriction within s 8(1) for courts to grant only remedies 'within their powers' include powers in common law and under statute.

11 Judicial acts

JUDICIAL IMMUNITY AND DAMAGES

11.1 In setting out the purpose of s 9, the Home Secretary, Jack Straw, explained—

'[Section] 9 serves two main functions. It preserves the general principle of judicial immunity when a court or tribunal is found, or alleged, to have acted in a way that is made unlawful by [section] 6, and it provides for the possibility of damages being awarded against the Crown in respect of a judicial act, to the extent necessary to comply with Article 5(5) of the Convention.'[1]

---

[1] HC 2R, 16 February 1998, col 781.

11.2 Courts and tribunals are public authorities for the purposes of HRA 1998 (s 6(3)(a): see further para 8.4) and hence it is unlawful for a court or tribunal to act in a manner which is incompatible with a Convention right, providing they could have not acted otherwise by virtue of primary legislation (s 6(1)). Accordingly, an action may be brought under s 7(1)(a) in relation to a 'judicial act', an act by a court or tribunal which failed to comply with the Convention rights (see paras 9.5–9.10). Remedies in respect of that act may be sought under s 8 (see Ch 10). Section 9 governs the manner of the proceedings by which such claims can be brought and the provision of damages in such cases.

11.3 Section 9, as originally drafted in the Bill, protected the Crown from liability in tort for judicial acts. It sought to preserve common law and statutory rules which broadly gave personal immunity from prosecution to judges and magistrates acting within their jurisdiction or acting in good faith outside their jurisdiction, for example Justices of the Peace Act 1997, Pt V, ss 51, 52. Lord Meston first raised the issue of the UK's obligations under Art 5(5) of the Convention during Committee in the House of Lords,[1] seeking to amend clause 9 to reflect the obligation imposed by Art 5(5) upon the UK to provide an enforceable right to compensation for those who have been unlawfully arrested or detained by a judicial act. Based on the Government's assurances that the matter would be considered further, Lord Meston withdrew his amendment. The Government, during the Report stage of the Bill in the House of Lords introduced an amended clause 9,[2] which fully reflected the UK's obligation under Art 5(5) of the Convention to provide an enforceable right to compensation for arrest or detention contrary to the provisions of Art 5.

---

[1] HL Committee, 24 November 1997, col 856.
[2] HL Report, 29 January 1998, col 388.

11.4 The Government introduced this amendment as follows—

'[The amendment] has two purposes. The first is to provide an enforceable right to compensation for breaches of Article 5 by judicial acts. The second is to preserve judicial immunity generally for judicial acts undertaken by judges, magistrates, tribunal members and court staff performing judicial functions or acting on behalf of the judge or on the instructions of the judge.

. . . The effect of [sections] 6, 7 and 8 of the [Act] is that there is an enforceable right to compensation in relation to public authorities generally. But special provisions are needed in relation to judicial acts of courts and tribunals.

Where a complaint is made that Article 5 has been breached as a result of a judicial act or omission it will be necessary first to establish whether the judicial act complained of was unlawful, then to rule on whether the aggrieved person is entitled to compensation under Article 5(5) and then to determine the amount of the compensation. In determining those questions the court will take into account the Strasbourg jusrisprudence on unlawful detention and on the award of damages, as required by [sections] 2 and 8 of the [Act].'[1]

---

[1]   The Lord Chancellor, Lord Irvine of Lairg: HL Report, 29 January 1998, col 389.

11.5 Lord Irvine provides a helpful analysis of the criteria that the courts should consider in dealing with claims that an individual's Art 5(5) rights have been violated by a judicial act. First, whether the judicial act was unlawful, secondly, whether there is an entitlement to compensation and thirdly, what guidelines ought to be considered when assessing the amount of damages to be awarded.

Definition of 'judicial acts'

11.6 A 'judicial act' is defined by s 9(5) as a judicial act of a court or tribunal, including an act done on the instructions, or on behalf, of a judge. Such acts would therefore include acts by magistrates, whether stipendiary or lay, acts of the court clerk and acts of any other officer formally authorised to exercise the court's jurisdiction. However, it is only the acts of a court or tribunal which are caught by the definition in s 9. Lord Irvine made clear in Parliament that s 9 is not intended to cover a situation such as, for example, a prison officer imposing a penalty on a prisoner in breach of prison rules.[1]

---

[1]   HL 3R, 5 February 1998, col 817.

THE FORUM FOR 'JUDICIAL ACT' CLAIMS

11.7 Section 9(1) restricts the type of proceedings under which a s 7(1)(a) claim in respect of a judicial act may be brought. Such claims may be brought only by exercising a right of appeal (s 9(1)(a)) or by an application for judicial review (in Scotland a 'petition') (s 9(1)(b)) or in any other forum as may be prescribed by rules (s 9(1)(c)). 'Rules' has the same meaning as that given in s 7(9).

11.8 Lord Irvine provided guidance during the Parliamentary debates on fora available under s 9(1) for s 7(1)(a) claims—

'A finding that an inferior court has acted unlawfully will most commonly be reached in England and Wales by way of appeal to the Court of Appeal or the Divisional Court, or by an application by way of judicial review to the High Court. The higher court will then be able to reach a decision of unlawfulness and make an award of damages. [Section] 8(2) will enable the courts, which already have power to award damages, to do so in proceedings under this [Act]. However, in criminal proceedings in Scotland, if the High Court on appeal finds that some act of an inferior court has contravened the complainant's rights under Article 5(5) it would have no power to award damages. It would therefore be necessary for the amount of damages to be determined by the civil courts. [Section 9(1)] therefore enables proceedings to be brought in such other forum as may be prescribed by the rules. The Court of Appeal in England, as a single entity, has the power to award damages. Rules will provide as to whether the Criminal or Civil Division should hear compensation claims. Again, [sections] 9(1) and 7(2) provide the necessary powers to make rules.'[1]

---

[1]   HL Report, 29 January 1998, col 389.

EXISTING RULE UPHELD

11.9   Section 9(2), according to Lord Irvine, 'underlines that no new right to judicial review is being created'[1] under s 9(1), by specifying that it does not affect any rule of law which prevents a court from being the subject of judicial review. Accordingly, the existing rule that there may be no judicial review in respect of trials on indictment is upheld. Challenges to a decision by a Crown Court in a matter relating to trial on indictment will continue to be made on appeal and not by a judicial review application or petition.

---

[1]   HL Report, 29 January 1998, col 390.

AWARD OF DAMAGES IN RESPECT OF JUDICIAL ACTS

11.10   Under s 9(3) damages are not available in relation to judicial acts done in good faith, 'otherwise than to compensate a person to the extent required by Art 5(5) of the Convention'. Thus, where a court or tribunal is found to have breached Art 5(5), which states that a person who has been arrested or detained in contravention of the Article shall have an enforceable right to compensation, damages may be awarded. The Government amended s 9(3) to provide an enforceable right to compensation for unlawful judicial acts. This represents a significant change to existing law. Lord Lester commented on this amendment during the Report stage of the Bill in the House of Lords—

'As I understand it, until the Courts and Legal Services Act 1990 came into force it was possible for someone who had been unlawfully detained by order of a magistrates' court to take civil proceedings against the relevant Bench of magistrates. In cases in which imprisonment was unlawful, compensation could be paid.

Sections 44 and 45 of the 1990 Act introduced a requirement for the plaintiff to allege and prove malice before compensation could be ordered. That in effect rendered such litigation impossible and ended the right to compensation for unlawful detention by a magistrates' court. The Strasbourg case law is that a requirement to prove malice as a precondition to compensation does not conform to Article 5(5) of the Convention. The amendment deals with that problem extremely well. It extends to a judicial act of a court done in good faith so that damages can be awarded to compensate a person to the extent required by Article 5(5). It impliedly repeals Sections 44 and 45 of the Courts and Legal Services Act.'[1]

[1]   HL Report, 29 January 1998, col 391.

DAMAGES AWARDED AGAINST THE CROWN

11.11   Section 9(4) provides that in the event of damages being awarded for breach of Art 5(5) by a judicial act, such damages shall be awarded against the Crown, but only where 'the appropriate person' has been joined to the proceedings. This phrase is defined as 'the Minister responsible for the court concerned, or a person or government department nominated by him' (s 9(5)). The reason for this is clearly to provide the Crown with an opportunity to make representations on the award of damages, although the section does not specify when the 'appropriate person' ought to be joined, nor whether notice must be given to the Crown where such an award is being considered. In the view of Lord Irvine—

'Subsection (4) provides that an award of damages permitted by subsection (3) should be made against the Crown rather than against the judge personally. It also ensures that whichever Minister is responsible for the court or tribunal concerned is joined to the proceedings if not already a party. This is similar in effect to the provision of [section] 5 which provides that where a court is considering whether to make a declaration of incompatibility, the Crown is entitled to notice and, on an application to the court, to be joined as the party to the proceedings. In practice, the Lord Chancellor will be the appropriate person in many cases concerning judges and magistrates, in England and Wales. In Scotland, the relevant Minister will usually be the Secretary of State. But there may be cases where the breach of the Article 5 provisions arises from a wholly proper judicial decision required by inconsistent legislation, primary or secondary legislation. In this case it would be helpful for the Minister responsible to be joined. 'Appropriate person' therefore allows me, or the Secretary of State for Scotland to nominate a person or government department.'[1]

[1]   HL Report, 29 January 1998, col 390.

12 Remedial action and remedial orders

REMEDIAL ACTION

12.1 The purpose of s 10 was explained by the Government as follows—

'[Section 10] allows a remedial order to be made to amend a piece of primary legislation so as to remove an incompatibility that has been found to exist in one of its provisions. [Schedule 2, para 1(1)(a)] provides that a remedial order under [section] 10 may contain such incidental, supplemental, consequential and transitional provisions as the person making it considers appropriate. [Schedule 2, para 1(2)(a)] provides that the power to make incidental changes includes power to amend or repeal primary legislation, including primary legislation other than that which contains the incompatible provision.'[1]

'We think that we have the right balance here. [Section] 10 and Schedule 2 enable Parliament to fulfil its responsibilities and ensure that onerous powers are not given to the Government.'[2]

---

[1] The Lord Chancellor, Lord Irvine of Lairg: HL Report, 29 January 1998, col 401.
[2] Mike O'Brien, Parliamentary Under-Secretary of State for the Home Department: HC Report, 21 October 1998, col 1331.

THE POWER TO TAKE REMEDIAL ACTION

12.2 The Home Secretary, Jack Straw, explained the reasons for including the power to take remedial action as follows—

'The power to make a remedial order exists for cases—we do not think there will be very many—when there is a very good reason to amend the law following a declaration of incompatibility or a finding by the Strasbourg Court, but no suitable legislative vehicle is available . . . [for example a] declaration of incompatibility might arise where the legislation in question had touched on the liberty of the subject . . . [and the higher court takes the view that] the rights of the subject spelled out in the Convention have been unjustifiably interfered with by the primary legislation of this Parliament. Therefore, a remedial order aims to restore, or to give to the subject for the first time, liberties that the subject had previously been denied by Parliament. In those cases, I believe that Parliament would wish to act swiftly, but it may well be that there was no criminal justice Bill before the House through which amendments could be made. In those circumstances, the power to make a specific and necessary amendments by means of a remedial order could be useful.'[1]

---

[1] HC Committee, 24 June 1998, col 1137.

12.3 Where a domestic court has made a declaration of incompatibility under s 4 of HRA 1998 and there will be no appeal against it (s 10(1)(a)) or where a violation of the Convention is found against the UK by the Strasbourg Court (s 10(1)(b)), a Minister of the Crown, or Her Majesty in Council with respect to Orders in Council (s 10(5)), may take remedial action to amend the domestic legislation concerned to address the incompatibility by order (s 10(3)). Primary legislation may be amended by virtue of s 10 by statutory instrument. This is a significant departure from the traditional legislative approach in the UK whereby primary legislation could only be amended by primary legislation. The Government has stated that the aim of s 10 is to provide a 'prompt parliamentary remedy'[1] to the two instances above, and the result is one of the most controversial aspects of the Act.

---

[1]   Lord Irvine: HL 2R, 3 November 1997, col 1231.

12.4 Section 10(1)(b) provides that the power to take remedial action applies if 'it appears to a Minister . . . or Her Majesty in Council that, having regard to a finding of the European Court of Human Rights made after the coming into force of this section in proceedings against the United Kingdom, a provision of legislation is incompatible with an obligation of the United Kingdom arising from the Convention.' Thus, remedial action by a Minister under s 10 is not authorised with respect to violations found by the Strasbourg Court against the UK prior to s 10 entering into force. Further, remedial action under s 10 is limited to where the UK has been found in violation of the Convention and does not extend to violations found against other States. (see para 4.8).

CONFLICTING LEGISLATION

12.5 A Minister is not compelled to take remedial action where legislation is found to be incompatible with the Convention—instead, the power conferred under s 10 is discretionary. In respect of domestic legislation, a Minister's powers can be used where the legislation is declared under s 4 to be incompatible with 'a Convention right' ie one of the rights enumerated in s 1(1), and where the appeal criteria in s 10(1)(a) have been satisfied (see para 12.9). In respect of a violation against the UK found by the Strasbourg Court, a Minister's powers can be used when there has been a finding that any of the rights of the Convention has been breached (see para 4.8).

12.6 The prospect of conferring such a power to amend primary legislation by subordinate legislation, ie by statutory instrument, upon a Minister, unsurprisingly provoked heated debate in Parliament.

12.7 Jack Straw promoted the remedial provisions under section 10 on behalf of the Government, stating—

> 'In the normal way, primary legislation can be amended only by further primary legislation. As we all know . . . that can take a long time. One of the consequences of not having a special procedure to remedy defects in legislation is a degree of paralysis. Until now, the remedy has been through the Strasbourg Court.[1]

... the purpose of remedial action is to try to resolve the current paralysis, which is to nobody's advantage. It is not to take away anyone's rights; it is to confer rights.[2]

One of the questions that will always be before Government, in practice, will be, 'Is it sensible to wait for a further challenge to Strasbourg, when the British courts have declared the provision to be outwith the Convention?'[3]

---

[1]   HC 2R, 16 February 1998, col 772.
[2]   Ibid, col 773.
[3]   Ibid, col 774.

12.8 Lord Lester also lent support to the s 10 powers as a speedy method by which incompatible legislation may be amended, emphasising the safeguards of parliamentary control enshrined within the Act—

'Some have criticised the power to take remedial action by subordinate legislation as being a sinister sapping of parliamentary powers. That criticism is misconceived. At present, when a judgment of the European Court requires the amendment of primary legislation, that can only be done by new, amending primary legislation. That is a slow and cumbersome method of complying with our international obligations. It has sometimes resulted in a tardy and incomplete implementation. Similarly, where a British court decides that there is a fatal inconsistency in a statute, what is needed is a speedy means of remedying the defect and of providing a remedy for the individual victim.

Under the European Communities Act 1972 ... the power to implement the UK's Community obligations may be implemented by subordinate legislation, without any requirement to obtain the affirmative approval of both Houses. But this [Act] provides for stronger parliamentary control, as, except in cases of pressing urgency, the implementation of the UK's Convention obligations by subordinate legislation can be done only by the affirmative procedure. To require the Government to introduce primary amending legislation to give effect to European or British judgments would be to hinder the speedy and effective implementation by Parliament of Convention rights, obligations and remedies.'[1]

---

[1]   HL 2R, 3 November 1997, col 1240.

Procedural requirements

12.9 In cases where a declaration of incompatibility under s 4 has been made (see Ch 6), the power to take remedial action becomes effective only when all persons who may appeal have stated in writing that they do not intend to do so (s 10(1)(a)), or the time for bringing an appeal has expired and no appeal has been brought (s 10(1)(b)) or an appeal has been brought within time and has been determined or abandoned (s 10(1)(c)). These requirements were added to guard against the possibility of legislation being amended by remedial order in response to a declaration of incompatibility which was then overturned on appeal. (See s 5 and the right to appeal against a declaration of incompatibility made in criminal proceedings at para 7.3).

'COMPELLING REASONS'

12.10   Section 10(2) provides: 'If a Minister of the Crown considers that there are *compelling reasons* for proceeding under this section, he may by order make such amendments to the legislation as he considers necessary to remove the incompatibility' [author's emphasis]. This is the crux of s 10 and the Minister's powers to amend primary legislation. As originally drafted, the section provided that a Minister could act to amend legislation under 10 where 'appropriate', but this was later amended to allay fears that s 10 might be used routinely by Ministers to amend primary legislation—

> 'We are deleting the word "appropriate" in [section] 10 and saying that a remedial order can be brought forward only if there are compelling reasons. We are setting a very high test. Only the changes necessary to remove the incompatibility will be possible.'[1]

---

[1]   Jack Straw: HC Committee, 24 June 1998, col 1138.

12.11   Mike O'Brien explained further the requirement for 'compelling reasons' to exist—

> 'The requirement for compelling reasons in [section] 10(2) is . . . there to make it absolutely clear that a remedial order is not a routine response in preference to fresh primary legislation . . . for example, a decision of the higher courts in relation to basic provisions of criminal procedure affecting the way in which, perhaps, all criminal cases must be handled. An example is a provision that might invalidate a crucial part of the codes of practice under the Police and Criminal Evidence Act 1984, or provisions relating to the detention of suspects . . . there are a number of issues where we would want to proceed with care. We might also need to respond very quickly simply to avoid the criminal justice system in such cases either collapsing or not being able to deliver justice and proper convictions.'[1]

---

[1]   HC Report, 21 October 1998, col 1330.

Definition of 'compelling'

12.13   During the debates, the Government was vague as to the meaning of the word 'compelling' for the purposes of s 10.[1] Mike O'Brien, for example, chose to give two examples of situations in which primary legislation would be 'expected', stating that—

> '"Compelling" is a strong word. We see no need to define it by reference to particular categories. . . . [on issues such as] electoral law and chastising children[,] everyone would expect primary legislation rather than a remedial order.'[2]

---

[1]   Jack Straw had given an even more vague reply to a question on 'compelling reasons' when questioned by Dominic Grieve in Committee—
'Mr Grieve: . . . I should be interested to hear . . . what the Home Secretary understands by "compelling" and how he would differentiate that from "exceptional" . . .

Mr Straw: I am answering ad lib and without the benefit of a legal dictionary, but the situation . . . in the Chahal case, where the liberty of a subject would be adversely affected by a delay in producing primary legislation, was a compelling case. I am not certain that it would be an exceptional case, because one could ask, "To what is it exceptional?" but it would certainly be a compelling case. Frankly, only in that situation would remedial orders be necessary and appropriate.' (HC Committee, 24 June 1998, col 1140).

2   HC Report, 21 October 1998, col 1330.

12.14   It could be inferred from this statement that it is the Government's opinion that the type of legislation is the determining factor, rather than the circumstances, which should be 'compelling' for the Minister concerned. However, the words of Jack Straw should be referred to, ie that the ever-present question for the Government is—'Is it sensible to wait for further challenge to Strasbourg, when the British courts have declared the provision to be outwith the Convention?'[1] Under s 10(2), this may be a question for the Minister to ask himself.

1   HC 2R, 16 February 1998, col 774.

SUBORDINATE LEGISLATION

12.15   Section 10(3) provides that if, in the case of subordinate legislation, the Minister considers that it is necessary to amend the primary legislation under which the subordinate legislation was made in order to remove the incompatibility (s 10(3)(a)) and if there are compelling reasons to do so (s 10(3)(b)), the Minister may by order amend the primary legislation.

12.16   Where a provision of subordinate legislation has been quashed, or declared invalid, by reason of incompatibility with a Convention right, a Minister may make a remedial order under s 10(4) in respect of that provision. This is limited, however, to where it appears to the Minister to be urgent to do so (Sch 2, para 2(b)). Since the provision will no longer be in force, it is unlikely that an 'urgent' situation would often arise where it would be necessary for the Minister to utilise this power.

CHURCH LEGISLATION

12.17   Section 10(6) provides that 'In this section "legislation" does not include a Measure of the Church Assembly or of the General Synod of the Church of England'. This clause was included because, as the previous draft clause stood, a Minister could make a remedial order, without any reference to the General Synod, amending a measure of the General Synod or of its predecessor, the Church Assembly, following a declaration of incompatibility.

12.18   Lord Williams of Mostyn, Under-Secretary of State at the Home Office, explained why it was felt necessary to remove Church legislation from the ambit of amendment by s 10 powers, referring to the existing arrangements of parliamentary approval of church measures—

'The Church of England, perfectly properly, pointed out that [to include Church legislation within section 10] would sit uneasily with our present arrangements whereby a Church measure can only be approved or disapproved by Parliament in its entirety—in other words, with no opportunity for amendment . . . we came to the conclusion that if an amendment to Church measures were required to remove a Convention incompatibility, it is better done by the Church itself rather than by the exercise of the order-making power by a Minister of the Crown.'[1]

---

[1]   HL Report, 29 January 1998, col 396.

REMEDIAL ORDERS

12.19   Schedule 2 of the 1998 Act contains provisions concerning form, content and procedure relating to remedial orders.

12.20   Under Sch 2, para 1(1)(a), a remedial order may 'contain such incidental, supplemental, consequential or transitional provision as the person making it considers appropriate'. It may include the power to amend primary legislation, including primary legislation other than that which contains the incompatible legislation (Sch 2, para 1(2)(a)), and it may include the power to amend or revoke subordinate legislation, again including subordinate legislation other than that which contains the incompatible provision (Sch 2, para 1(2)(b)). The remedial order may be made so as to have the same extent as the legislation which it affects (Sch 2, para 1(3)). No person is to be guilty of an offence solely as a result of the retrospective effect of a remedial order (Sch 2, para 1(4)). Under s 7(8) nothing in the 1998 Act creates a criminal offence (see para 9.22), however, amendments may be made to criminal legislation, as with any other legislation except church legislation, by a remedial order under the 1998 Act. The inclusion of Sch 2, para 1(4), in line with s 7(8), protects from retrospective effect any person affected by such changes made to domestic criminal law.

12.21   Schedule 2, para 2, prescribes the two conditions in which a remedial order may be made. The first instance is where an order has been laid in draft and then approved after 60 days by a resolution of each House of Parliament. The 60 day period commences on the day on which the draft was made (Sch 2, para 2(a)). The second is where, because of the urgency of the matter, 'it is declared in the order that it appears to the person making it that . . . it is necessary to make the order without a draft being so approved' (Sch 2, para 2(b)). Thus, a remedial order which has not been approved in draft must contain a declaration of the urgency.

Scrutiny of orders laid in draft

12.22   The 1998 Act does not include provision for amendment by Parliament of the draft order laid before it under Sch 2, para 2(a). Parliament may either approve the draft order or decline to approve it. Schedule 2, para 3 provides a procedure by which parliamentary scrutiny may take place before the draft is laid.

12.23   The procedure under Sch 2, para 3 provides that a document containing a draft of the proposed order must be laid before Parliament (Sch 2, para 3(1)(a)). This document must also include 'the required information', defined in Sch 2, para 5 as 'an explanation of the incompatibility which the order (or proposed order) seeks to remove, including particulars of the relevant declaration, finding or order' and 'a statement of the reasons for proceeding under section 10 and for making an order in those terms'. The requirement to provide a document containing all the relevant information was added during the deliberations of the House of Commons in Committee. Mike O'Brien explained the importance of the document, stating that it—

> '. . . must explain the incompatibility that the remedial order or draft remedial order seeks to remove, and it must state the reasons for proceeding under [section] 10 and for making an order in the terms in which it is made.
>
> Therefore, the document is bound to explain why the Government believe that there are compelling reasons for making a remedial order and what those are. The document must be laid before Parliament and will be available for the debate in each House on the motion for affirmative resolution, which will be necessary before a draft remedial order can be made, or in order for an urgent remedial order to continue in existence . . .
>
> . . .
>
> The power to make a remedial order is there for cases where there is a very good reason to amend the law following a declaration of incompatibility or a finding by the Strasbourg court, but no suitable legislative vehicle is available. Where a remedial order is made or proposed, we accepted that the procedures for parliamentary scrutiny needed to be strengthened. That is why the requirement to provide a document containing all the relevant information and a statement providing a summary of any representations on an order or a draft order was added to Schedule 2 in Committee.'[1]

---

[1] HC Report, 21 October 1998, col 1330.

12.24 As required by Sch 2, para 3(1)(b) this document must be laid before Parliament for 60 days. If any representations are made during that time, a statement must be affixed to the draft order laid under Sch 2, para 2(a), containing a summary of the representations and details of any changes made to the proposed order (see para 12.30).

12.25 Thus, any draft remedial order under Sch 2, para 2(a) will lie before Parliament for a total of 120 days before it can take effect as a remedial order, first, contained within a document for 60 days as a proposed draft, and then for a further 60 days as a final draft awaiting approval by both Houses of Parliament. This is the most stringent affirmative resolution procedure available for statutory instruments.

URGENT CASES: SAFEGUARDS

12.26 Schedule 2, para 4 provides safeguards concerning parliamentary scrutiny following a remedial order being made under Sch 2, para 2(b), unapproved by Parliament by reason of the urgency of the situation but which has taken immediate effect.

12.27   Under Sch 2, para 4(1) if a remedial order is made without being approved in draft, the person making it must lay it before Parliament, accompanied by 'the required information', after it is made (see para 12.23). Sch 2, para 4(2) provides that if, within 60 days of the remedial order being made, representations have been made, once that period of 60 days expires a statement must be laid before Parliament (see para 12.30). This must contain a summary of the representations (para 4(2)(a)) and any changes to the original order thereby considered appropriate (para 4(2)(b)). In the latter event, where changes are made to the remedial order in consequence of representations, Sch 2, para 4(3) applies, requiring the person who made the statement to make a further remedial order replacing the original one. That replacement order must then be laid before Parliament.

12.28   Schedule 2, para 4(4) lays down the time limit by which the remedial/replacement order must be approved by Parliament. If 120 days elapse from the date the original remedial order was laid before Parliament without each House of Parliament either approving the original or the replacement order, the order ceases to have effect. The cessation of the order will not, however, affect 'anything previously done under either order or the power to make a fresh remedial order'.

12.29   Whereas draft remedial orders laid under Sch 2, para 2(a) have to be approved in their entirety and are not subject to amendment by Parliament, in the case of urgent remedial orders under Sch 2, para 2(b), a replacement order is permissible. This no doubt relates to the fact that the urgent remedial order will have already taken effect and thus in such circumstances the possibility of amendment should not be ruled out. Nonetheless, both types of remedial order must be able to obtain the approval of both Houses of Parliament, or they will fail.

REPRESENTATIONS

12.30   As explained at paras 12.24, 12.27, representations may be made within the 60 day period during which a proposed order under Sch 2, para 3 or an urgent remedial order under Sch 2, para 4 lies before Parliament. 'Representations' are defined in Sch 2, para 5 as 'representations about a remedial order (or proposed remedial order) made to the person making (or proposing to make) it and includes any relevant Parliamentary report or resolution'. This is an inclusive definition, and public interest groups and representative groups, for example, ought to be prompted during this time to put forward representations of their own to the Government Minister in charge of making the order.

CALCULATING WHEN TIME IS TO RUN

12.31   In calculating any periods of time outlined above for remedial orders, no account is to be taken of time during which Parliament is dissolved or prorogued (Sch 2, para 6(a)), or where both Houses are adjourned for more than four days (Sch 2, para 6(b)).

13 Safeguard for existing human rights

EXISTING RIGHTS

13.1 Lord Williams of Mostyn, Under-Secretary of State at the Home Office, provided an explanation as to the inclusion of s 11 in the 1998 Act— '[Section 11] . . . is simply to provide a saving for other human rights. It is there to ensure that if a person has existing rights, nothing in this [Act] shall detract from them in any way . . . '.[1]

---

[1]   HL Report, 29 January 1998, col 410.

13.2 Under s 11(a) a person's reliance on a Convention right does not restrict any existing rights or freedoms that he enjoys under any UK law. In the words of the Lord Chancellor, Lord Irvine of Lairg, 'The purpose of [the] provision is to ensure that the [Act] gives but does not take away.'[1] Further, s 11(b) provides that a person's reliance on a Convention right does not restrict 'his right to make any claim or bring any proceedings which he *could* make or bring apart from sections 7 to 9' of the 1998 Act [author's emphasis]. Section 11(b) places on a statutory footing the right of an individual to rely on future rights which may be developed by Parliament or via the common law.

---

[1]   HL Committee, 27 November 1997, col 1157.
[1]   See Ch 9 in relation to s 7 claims and Ch 11 in relation to s 9 claims.

13.3 Clause 13 (now s 11), was amended to include the safeguard now contained within s 11(b) during the Report stage of the Bill in the House of Lords. Lord Lester explained the importance of the amendment, namely that it—

' . . . makes clear that which is already implicit in the Bill—namely, that the European Convention contains a floor of minimum rights guaranteed under international law, but does not create a ceiling. Therefore, if Parliament chooses to go further or if the common law goes further in protecting our basic rights and freedoms, which are inherent in us as citizens and human beings, the Convention and the Bill are not to restrict that. The fact that that is a minimum and not a maximum is made clear in the Convention itself. It does not mean that there will never be conflict and difficult questions to be resolved as a result of people arguing that, say, the Race Relations Act is an infringement of some basic right in the Convention, or other such points. It is important that one does not concentrate only upon the Convention as a guarantee of rights. As the amendment makes clear, the common law will continue to develop in a creative way and no doubt the Convention will be used, as the Bill makes clear, in the course of developing the common law.

I . . . believe that one should approach Convention rights through our common law and through the statute book, not round the common law or the statute book . . . one intertwines Convention rights into our domestic legal system. One of the many virtues of the Bill is the fact that those who have thought it through and drafted it have found ways to create very subtle connections between Convention rights and our own statute law and common law.'[1]

---

[1]   HL Report, 29 January 1998, col 410.

13.4 Lord Lester's reference to the Convention providing a 'floor' of minimum guarantees for human rights is reflected within the Convention itself. The Convention draftsmen made express provision for safeguarding existing human rights by including the following—

'Nothing in this Convention shall be construed as limiting or derogating from any of the human rights and fundamental freedoms which may be ensured under the laws of any High Contracting Party or under any other agreement to which it is a Party.'[1]

---

[1]   Article 53 of the Convention, as amended by Protocol 11, which entered into force on 1 November 1998.

14 Freedom of expression

SAFEGUARDS

14.1 Section 12 provides a variety of safeguards relating to the right of freedom of expression, which is protected by Art 10 of the Convention. Concern was voiced during Parliamentary debate on the Bill by some MPs and the press that the traditional exercise of freedom of expression under domestic law might be curtailed by the sometimes opposing right to privacy under Art 8 of the Convention. The concern centred mainly on fears that HRA 1998 might undermine press freedom and introduce a privacy law via the back door. In response to these fears, the Bill was amended to include the safeguards contained within s 12. The Home Secretary, Jack Straw, stated the Government's position—'We have taken the opportunity to enhance press freedom in a wider way than would arise simply from the incorporation of the Convention into our domestic law.'[1]

---

[1]   HC Committee, 2 July 1998, col 536.

14.2 A domestic court or tribunal considering whether to grant any relief which may affect the exercise of freedom of expression (s 12(1)) must have particular regard to the importance of that freedom (s 12(4)). This direction to domestic courts departs from the approach taken by the Commission and Court in Strasbourg, where, in cases involving competing rights under Arts 8 and 10, the outcome reflects a balancing act, particular to the facts of an individual case. However, since the domestic courts are required under s 2 of the 1998 Act to take relevant Strasbourg case law into account, whenever a question of an Art 10 right is raised, in practice, the courts will be required to consider the case law on Art 8 matters alongside Art 10 issues.

14.3 The 1998 Act purports to give Art 10 a special significance in domestic law. This must be borne in mind whenever a court is deciding whether to grant a remedy which might affect the right to freedom of expression. Accordingly, such a consideration may be required where an injunction is sought against a newspaper restraining publication, and even in defamation proceedings between private individuals. 'It applies to the press, broadcasters or anyone whose right to freedom of expression might be affected. It is not limited to cases to which a public authority is a party.'[1] The only instance in which the court is exempted from its duty under s 12 is when considering granting relief in criminal proceedings (s 12(5)).

---

[1]   Jack Straw: HC Committee, 2 July 1998, col 536.

PROCEEDINGS IN THE ABSENCE OF THE RESPONDENT

14.4 Section 12(2) provides that no relief is to be granted where the respondent is absent or unrepresented, except where the court is satisfied that the applicant has taken all practicable steps to notify the respondent (s 12(2)(a)) or where there are compelling reasons why the respondent should not be notified (s 12(2)(b)). Discussing s 12(2)(a), Jack Straw explained that—

> 'The courts are well able to deal with the first limb of that exception relating to whether all practical steps have been taken to notify the respondent, and in the case of broadcasting authorities and the press, rarely would the applicant not be able to serve notice of the proceedings on the respondent.'[1]

---

[1]   HC Committee, 2 July 1998, col 536.

14.5 In discussing s 12(2)(b), whereby a court must be satisfied that 'compelling reasons' exist in order to grant a remedy in the absence of the respondent, Jack Straw continued—

> 'The latter circumstance—compelling reasons—might arise in a case raising issues of national security where the mere knowledge that an injunction was being sought might cause the respondent to publish the material immediately. We do not anticipate that that limb would be used often. In the past, such applications have been rare, but there has been at least one recent case involving the Ministry of Defence.
>
> . . . the provision is intended overall to ensure that ex parte injunctions are granted only in exceptional circumstances. Even where both parties are represented, we expect that injunctions will continue to be rare, as they are at present.'[1]

---

[1]   HC Committee, 2 July 1998, col 536.

'FRIDAY NIGHT INJUNCTIONS'

14.6 Under HRA 1998, no relief will be granted to restrain publication before trial unless the court is satisfied that the applicant is likely to succeed at trial, ie that the applicant is 'likely to establish that publication should not be allowed' (s 12(3)). This provision was incorporated into the 1998 Act to allay the fears of publishers that interim injunctions, commonly termed in the publishing trade as 'Friday night injunctions', might simply be granted to preserve the status quo, pending a full determination of the application at a later hearing by which time the proposed story might not be newsworthy.

14.7 Section 12(3) requires a court to consider the merits of the application at the interlocutory stage, and represents a departure from the established test stated in *American Cyanamid Co v Ethicon Ltd 1975*, namely that there be proven 'a serious question to be tried'.[1] In cases involving the effect of a remedy on freedom of expression, the courts will now have to return to the pre-American Cyanamid position, where they had to consider the respective merits of the parties cases in some detail. Successful applications for such 'Friday night injunctions', which raise a question of freedom of expression, will undoubtedly become rare, not least for the impracticality of having to prepare and file at the last minute detailed affidavits to establish a prima facie case on the merits. As Jack Straw commented—

'. . . it is already difficult to get interlocutory relief. We are in a sense reinforcing that difficulty, for good reasons that I wholly defend, because of the importance of protecting the right to freedom of expression against other rights.

. . . we believe that the new clause would protect a respondent potential publisher from what amounts to legal or legalised intimidation . . . It will be very difficult to get [interlocutory relief] unless the applicant can satisfy the court that the applicant is likely to establish that publication should not be allowed. That is a much higher test than that there should simply be a prima facie case to get the matter into court.'[2]

---

[1]   [1975] AC 396.
[2]   HC Committee, 2 July 1998, col 537.

PROCEEDINGS INVOLVING JOURNALISTIC, LITERARY OR ARTISTIC MATERIAL

14.8   Under s 12(4) 'the courts must have particular regard to the importance of the Convention right to freedom of expression' (see paras 14.2, 14.3). Section 12(4) provides further directions to the court when the proceedings concern journalistic, literary or artistic material. Where the proceedings concern such material, or conduct related to such material,[1] the court must also have particular regard to the extent of any prior publication and the extent to which publication would be in the 'public interest' (s 12(4)(a)). On the definition of 'in the public interest' Jack Straw stated that—

'The courts are well versed in making judgments about the balance between a private interest of an applicant before them and the wider public interest.'[2]

and similarly—

'If the court and the parties to the proceedings know that a story will be published anyway, for example, in another country or on the internet, that must affect the decision whether it is appropriate to restrain publication by the print or the broadcast media in this country.'[3]

---

[1]   '. . . The reference in the new clause to 'conduct connected with such material' is intended for cases where journalistic inquiries suggest the presence of a story, but no actual material yet exists—perhaps because the story has not yet been written.' HC Committee, 2 July 1998, col 540.
[2]   HC Committee, 2 July 1998, col 539.
[3]   Ibid, col 538.

Privacy codes

14.9   Section 12(4)(b) provides that where the proceedings relate to journalistic, literary or artistic material, the courts must have particular regard to 'any relevant privacy code'. Jack Straw stated—

'Depending on the circumstances, that could be the newspaper industry code of practice operated by the Press Complaints Commission, the

Broadcasting Standards Commission code, the Independent Television
Commission code, or a broadcaster's internal code such as that operated
by the BBC. The fact that a newspaper has complied with the terms of
the code operated by the PCC—or conversely that it has breached the
code—is one of the factors that we believe the courts should take into
account in considering whether to grant relief.'[1]

---

[1]   HC Committee, 2 July 1998, col 538.

14.10   Newspapers owned by private individuals would thus be well-advised to
adopt a privacy code for the simple reason of being able to benefit from the
'protection' provided by s 12(4)(b).

THE EXEMPTION OF CRIMINAL PROCEEDINGS

14.11   By virtue of s 12(5) 'relief' includes any remedy or order other than those in
criminal proceedings. The reason for this exemption was explained by Jack Straw—

'We drafted the amendment with civil, rather than criminal, proceedings
against the media in mind. Without such an exclusion, judges wanting
to impose reporting restrictions in a criminal trial would, for example,
have to consider any relevant privacy code, although plainly it would not
be appropriate in that context . . . The special provision that we are
making in [section 12] does not therefore exempt criminal courts from
the general obligations imposed by other provisions of the [Act].
However, had we included criminal proceedings under [section 12], we
would have made the running of criminal trials very complicated.'[1]

---

[1]   HC Committee, 2 July 1998, col 540.

15 Freedom of thought, conscience and religion

COURT'S REQUIREMENT TO CONSIDER RELIGIOUS RIGHTS

15.1 Section 13(1) provides that if a court or tribunal's determination of any question arising under HRA 1998 might 'affect the exercise by a religious organisation (itself or its members collectively) of the Convention right to freedom of thought, conscience and religion', the court must have particular regard to the importance of that right.

15.2 The application of s 13 differs from s 12 which relates to freedom of expression. Under s 13, the court must take into account the right to freedom of thought, conscience and religion (protected by Art 9 of the Convention) at all stages of the proceedings where such a right might be affected, and not merely at the point where relief is being considered.

CONCERNS OF THE CHURCH

15.3 The amendments to HRA 1998 which related to religious rights were approved by the House of Lords during Third Reading in response to concerns voiced by the churches concerning, for example, the appointment of the clergy and the administration of marriages and of church schools.[1] The concerns stemmed from the prospect of the churches being deemed to be 'public authorities' under s 6(3)(b), as they are bodies certain of whose functions are of a public nature. However, as such they will be liable under HRA 1998 only for their public functions, and not their private acts, a distinction which became blurred during the extensive debates which took place concerning the liability of churches under the Act. Lord Lester, amongst others, sought to allay some of the churches' fears—

> '. . . the European Convention on Human Rights is a charter of religious tolerance and freedom, and has been so interpreted consistently by the European Court of Human Rights in upholding pluralism and religious freedom: for example, in refusing to extend the law of blasphemy in this country to protect other faiths in a way that would be an engine of intolerance, according to the European Human Rights Commission; and in refusing persistently to permit the taxation of churches in other countries, and in other ways showing complete respect for, as I say, religious intolerance and freedom, including the freedom of the Church of England of this country.'[2]

---

[1] HL 3R, 5 February 1998, cols 747–760, 770–790.
[2] HL Committee, 24 November 1997, col 799.

15.4 The Home Secretary, Jack Straw, sought to provide clarity on the difference between public functions and private acts, with particular reference to the private acts of churches that would not attract liability under HRA 1998—

'In the debate of 20 May this year, I stated:

'the regulation of divine worship . . . the administration of the sacrament, admission to Church membership or to the priesthood'

—obviously the term 'admission' covers non-admission and exclusion—

'are in our judgment, all private matters'—[HC Committee, 20 May 1998, col 1015]'.[1]

---

[1]   HC Report, 21 October 1998, col 1368.

15.5 Section 13 is intended to allay any concerns that the churches had in relation to duties which they might have been forced to perform under the 1998 Act, by providing that whenever a court is faced with issues arising under Art 9 of the Convention, it must have due regard to the importance of the rights protected. This will in practice add nothing more to the extensive protection of the Art 9 rights under Strasbourg case law.

16 Derogations and reservations

THE UK DEROGATION AND RESERVATION

16.1 HRA 1998 lists the Articles which are to be termed 'the Convention rights' (s 1(1)), and provides that 'Those Articles are to have effect for the purposes of this Act subject to any designated derogation or reservation (as to which see sections 14 and 15)' (s 1(2)). Sections 14 and 15 deal with the 'designated derogation' and the designated reservation' respectively. Section 16 provides a period for which designated derogations are to have effect, and s 17 provides for periodic review of designated reservations.

DESIGNATED DEROGATIONS AND DESIGNATED RESERVATIONS

16.2 Sections 14 and 15 of the 1998 Act place on a statutory footing the UK's current derogation from Art 5(3) of the Convention and its reservation to Art 2 of the First Protocol to the Convention. The derogation under Art 5(3) is set out in HRA 1998, Sch 3, Pt I and relates to the period of detention permitted for those suspected of terrorist offences in Northern Ireland. The reservation to Art 2 of the First Protocol to the Convention relates to the provision of education and is set out in Sch 3, Pt II.

16.3 HRA 1998, s 14(1) provides that a 'designated derogation' means the UK's derogation from Art 5(3) of the Convention and any future derogation entered into by the UK of the Convention or of any protocol thereto which is designated for the purposes of the 1998 Act by order of the Secretary of State. By virtue of s 14(6) a 'designation order may be made in anticipation of the making by the United Kingdom of a proposed derogation'.

16.4 Section 15(1) provides that a 'designated reservation' means the UK's reservation to Art 2 of the First Protocol to the Convention and any future reservation to the Convention or its protocols so designated by order of the Secretary of State. HRA 1998, Sch 3, Pt II contains the UK's current reservation, by which the UK accepts the obligation to guarantee to everyone the right to education 'only so far as it is compatible with the provision of efficient instruction and training, and the avoidance of unreasonable public expenditure.' Under s 15(5) the Secretary of State may make amendments to the 1998 Act to reflect any designation order, or to amend the effect of any reservation being withdrawn. Currently by virtue of s 15(3) if a designated reservation is withdrawn wholly or in part, it ceases to be a designated reservation, although under s 15(4) the Secretary of State may make a fresh designation order in respect of the Article concerned.

THE DURATION OF DESIGNATED DEROGATIONS

16.5 Article 15(1) of the Convention permits a State Party to take measures derogating from its obligations under the Convention in times of war or other public emergency 'to the extent strictly required by the exigencies of the situation, provided that such measures are not inconsistent with its other obligations under international law.' Under Art 15(2) no derogation from Art 2, except in respect of deaths resulting from lawful acts of war, or from Arts 3, 4(1) and 7 is permitted.

16.6 By virtue of Art 15(3) a State which adopts a derogation from the Convention obligations is required to keep the Secretary General of the Council of Europe informed of the measures which it has taken and the reasons for such measures. The State is also required to inform the Secretary General when it has ceased to operate such measures. The need to derogate from the Convention is considered to be a temporary measure, reflected in UK law for the first time by s 16 of the 1998 Act which provides a five-year period for designated derogations to have effect, subject to an extension of a further five years under s 16(2) upon the approval of both Houses of Parliament (see further para 16.8 on the nature of a derogation). An order by the Secretary of State which designates a new derogation under s 14(1)(b) must be approved by a resolution of both Houses of Parliament within 40 days of the order being laid for consideration (s 16(5)). If not so approved, the order ceases to have effect (s 16(3)). Where a designated derogation is withdrawn by the UK, the Secretary of State must by order make amendments to HRA 1998 to reflect that withdrawal (s 16(7)).

REVIEWS OF THE DESIGNATED RESERVATION

16.7 HRA 1998, s 17 provides that the appropriate Minister must, before the expiry of five years beginning with the date on which s 1(2) enters into force, review the designated reservation to Art 2 of the First Protocol and prepare a report on the result of that review. A copy of this report must be laid before each House of Parliament (s 17(3)). The Secretary of State under s 16(2) is given an express power to extend the designated derogation, whereas for an appropriate minister under s 17 this power is absent. However, the terminology of s 17(1) implies that it is not necessary for a formal extension to take place of the designated reservation. It will simply continue, with review reports being required every five years.

16.8 Article 57 of the Convention permits a State to enter into a reservation in respect of any particular provision of the Convention 'to the extent that any law then in force in its territory is not in conformity with the provision.' Reservations of a general nature are not permitted. While an obligation under Art 57(2) for any reservation should contain a brief statement of the law concerned, there is no duty to provide the Council of Europe with detailed reasoning as to why a State is entering into that particular reservation, unlike Art 15 derogations. This is clear when the wording of the UK's current derogation is compared to the wording of the UK's current reservation—both set out in Sch 3. The UK's current reservation was entered into in 1953, upon ratifying the First Protocol.

PARLIAMENTARY APPROVAL OF ORDERS

16.9 By virtue of HRA 1998, s 20(3) any statutory instrument made under ss 14, 15 or 16(7) must be laid before Parliament.

17 The appointment of judges to the European Court of Human Rights

THE APPOINTMENT OF JUDGES

17.1 Article 20 of the European Convention on Human Rights provides that—'The Court shall consist of a number of judges equal to that of the High Contracting Parties'. Thus, one appointee from each State which has ratified the Convention shall sit as a judge on the Strasbourg Court.

17.2 HRA 1998, s 18(2) provides that the holder of a judicial office may become a judge of the European Court of Human Rights. Where an appointment to that Court is made, the appointee will not be required to relinquish his or her judicial office at home (s 18(2)). This provision acts as a modification to the position prior to HRA 1998, where a serving judge had to resign his office if elected to the Strasbourg Court. In the Government's view—'We take the view that obligatory resignation might well dissuade potentially good candidates from coming forward when the office of UK judge to the Strasbourg Court has to be filled.'[1]

---

[1]   The Lord Chancellor, Lord Irvine of Lairg: HL Committee, 27 November 1997, col 1160.

17.3 The appointee will not, however, be required to carry out his judicial duties at home whilst being a judge of the Strasbourg Court (s 18(3)).

17.4 'Judicial office' for the purposes of the section is defined as the office of—
   (a) Lord Justice of Appeal (s 18(1)(a));
   (b) Justice of the High Court or Circuit Judge in England and Wales (s 18(1)(a));
   (c) judge of the Court of Session or sheriff in Scotland (s 18(1)(b));
   (d) Lord Justice of Appeal, judge of the High Court or county court judge in Northern Ireland (s 18(1)(c)).

17.5 The requirement under the 1998 Act that an appointee from the UK as a Strasbourg judge must be a holder of a 'judicial office' as defined in s 18 is distinct from the criteria for office contained in Art 21 of the Convention, which permits a broader category also to be considered for appointment. Article 21 provides that 'judges shall be of high moral character and must either possess the qualifications required for appointment to high judicial office or be jurisconsults of recognised competence'. It is also notable that Lords of Appeal in Ordinary do not hold 'judicial office' for the purposes of s 18.

17.6 Judges of the Strasbourg Court are paid by the Council of Europe, and this is reflected in s 18(4) which provides that domestic provisions for the payment of a salary to a UK judge will not apply to an appointee to the Court for the duration of their Strasbourg appointment. In addition provisions have been made to deal with the issue of pensions (s 18(6), Sch 4). Section 18(5) contains provisions relating to the appointment of a sheriff principal from Scotland to the Strasbourg Court, while s 18(7) provides for transitional provisions to be made by order of the Lord Chancellor or Secretary of State concerning the completion of service of a Strasbourg judge (see para 19.2).

JUDICIAL PENSIONS (SCH 4)

17.7 Schedule 4 deals with judicial pensions and imposes upon the appropriate Minister a duty to make orders about 'pensions payable to or in respect of any holder of a judicial office who serves as an ECHR judge' (Sch 4, para 1(1): see also para 19.2). The 'appropriate Minister' will be the Lord Chancellor, except in relation to any judicial office whose jurisdiction is exercisable exclusively in relation to Scotland, where it will be the Secretary of State (Sch 4, para 4). The imposition of a specific duty upon the Minister to order arrangements about pensions for a UK judge in Strasbourg is novel.

17.8 Schedule 4 provides favourable terms covering eligibility for a judicial pension and contributions towards it, drafted with the six-year period of appointment of a Strasbourg judge in mind. Ordinarily, Strasbourg judges will be elected for a six-year period and may be re-elected (Art 23), although the terms of half of the judges elected at the first election will expire at the end of three years. This is to ensure that the need to re-elect all the judges simultaneously after the first term of appointment does not arise. Any pensions order made must allow a judge who has been a member of a judicial pension scheme to remain in that scheme and his pension should be paid as if he had not had a period of service at the Strasbourg Court. Entitlement to benefits shall be calculated in accordance with the salary of the UK office which the judge holds (Sch 4, para 1(2)).

17.9 The pensions order may also contain provisions relating to contributions towards dependants' benefits which are payable by the UK judge. Alternative arrangements will have to be made by order to reflect the fact that whilst such contributions are normally deducted from the judicial salary received by a judge, the UK judge serving in Strasbourg will not be receiving a salary in the UK (Sch 4, para 2). A power also exists to amend relevant judicial pension legislation in order to facilitate the proper administration of a pensions scheme (Sch 4, para 3). Lord Irvine was very clear as to the objective which lay behind these provisions, particularly the provisions stating that time shall run for a pension during the term of appointment to Strasbourg— 'I believe that this will remove what might have been a powerful disincentive for some of our most able and highly qualified candidates from the judiciary to seek appointment to the ECHR.'[1]

---

[1]　HL Report, 29 January 1998, col 413.

17.10　By virtue of s 22(2), s 18 came into force on the day the 1998 Act received Royal Assent, namely 9 November 1998.

18 Pre-legislative scrutiny and statements of compatibility

IMPLICATIONS OF REQUIREMENTS UNDER s 19

18.1 As the Lord Chancellor, Lord Irvine of Lairg, explained during the Committee in the House of Lords—

> '[Section] 19 in itself is a very large gesture, as well as being a point of substance, in favour of the development of a culture of awareness of what the Convention requires in relation to domestic legislation.

> And so, by requiring the Minister in charge of a Bill to give a statement about its compatibility, we are underlining our commitment to undertaking further pre-legislative scrutiny of all new policy measures . . . Also, where the Minister states that he is unable to give a positive statement about the Bill's compatibility, that will be a very early signal to Parliament that the possible human rights implications of the Bill will need and will receive very careful consideration. Therefore, a statement giving the Government's conclusions, whether positive or negative, on the status of the Bill will go a long way towards the achievement of those aims.'[1]

---

[1] HL Committee, 27 November 1997, col 1163.

18.2 Under s 19(1) of the 1998 Act a Minister of the Crown in charge of a Bill emanating from either House of Parliament is required to make a statement to the effect that the Bill is in his view 'compatible with the Convention rights (a "statement of compatibility")' (s 19(1)(a)). Alternatively the Minister must 'make a statement to the effect that although he is unable to make a statement of compatibility the government nevertheless wishes the House to proceed with the Bill' (s 19(1)(b)). Such statements must be made prior to the Bill's Second Reading in both Houses.

18.3 Section 19(2) provides the form which either statement must take: it must be in writing, and must be published in such manner as the Minister considers appropriate. There is, however, no requirement for details to be given in the statement as to why the Bill is considered to be compatible or, conversely, reasons as to why the Government wishes to proceed in the absence of a confirmation of compatibility. Such a requirement, Lord Irvine argued, was unnecessary—

> 'Of course, Parliament will wish to know the reasons why the Government have taken whatever view they have taken, Therefore, I can understand why these amendments have been put forward. But the reasoning behind a statement of compatibility or the inability to make such a statement will inevitably be discussed by Parliament during the passage of the Bill. Of course it will be; and it will be discussed thoroughly.

> I believe that a debate in Parliament provides the best forum in which the Government's thinking can be fully explained.'[1]

[1]   HL Committee, 27 November 1997, col 1163.

18.4 During the latter stages of parliamentary consideration of the Human Rights Bill, Mike O'Brien, Parliamentary Under-Secretary of State for the Home Department, was asked for some examples of where a s 19(1)(b) statement might be made and when the Government might wish to proceed with a Bill that was not compatible with the Convention. Mike O'Brien replied—

> 'One example would be if we were legislating on the length of time for which the Secretary of State might authorise the detention of terrorist suspects under the Prevention of Terrorism (Temporary Provisions) Acts. The Strasbourg Court found our court in breach of Article 5 of the Convention some years ago, but we have maintained the arrangements because of the situation in Northern Ireland through a derogation as set out in Schedule 3 of the [Act].
>
> . . . we may properly want to proceed with a Bill that is incompatible with the Convention, although that will be rare and exceptional.'[1]

[1]   HC Report, 21 October 1998, col 1351.

18.5 The obligation to provide a statement under s 19 is joined to a requirement for the Minister in charge of the Bill to undertake proper and thorough pre-legislative scrutiny of Bills. Where a Minister has provided a s 19(1)(a) statement attesting that a Bill's provisions are 'compatible' with Convention rights prior to Second Reading, and there is later a declaration of incompatibility under s 4 in respect of that Act the consequences will be severe—

> 'If a Minister's prior assessment of compatibility (under [section 19(1)(a)]) is subsequently found by declaration of incompatibility to have been mistaken, it is hard to see how a Minister could withhold remedial action.'[1]

[1]   Lord Irvine, HL 2R, 3 November 1997, col 1229. See Ch 12 for commentary on remedial action, which is provided for in HRA 1998, s 10, Sch 2.

18.6 It is worth noting that the obligation upon a Minister to confirm whether or not legislation is compatible with Convention rights is one limited only to Bills proceeding through Parliament, ie to matters concerning primary legislation. There is no such obligation contained within the 1998 Act in respect of secondary or delegated legislation. Further no such obligation applies to Private Member's Bills.

18.7 The Human Rights Act 1998 (Commencement) Order 1998, SI 1998/2882, brought s 19 into force on 24 November 1998.

19 Supplemental provisions

ORDERS ETC UNDER THE ACT

19.1 Section 20 relates to the making of orders under the Act by a Minister, the Lord Chancellor or the Secretary of State. Any power of a Minister to make an order under the Act is exercisable by statutory instrument (s 20(1)).

19.2 Under s 20(2) the power of the Lord Chancellor or the Secretary of State to make rules (other than rules of court) under ss 2(3)[1] or 7(9)[2] is exercisable by statutory instrument. However, s 20(5) provides that any such statutory instrument shall be subject to annulment following a resolution of either House of Parliament. In addition, any statutory instrument made under s 18(7), (orders for transitional provisions relating to the completion of service of the appointed judge of the Strasbourg Court) or Sch 4 (orders relating to judicial pensions) shall be subject to annulment on the same terms.

---

[1] Rules relating to submitting evidence in domestic proceedings of any judgment, decision, declaration or opinion of the European Court or Commission of Human Rights or the Committee of Ministers.

[2] Rules determining which courts and tribunals are to be the appropriate forum for the hearing of claims that a public authority has acted 'unlawfully' for the purposes of the Act.

19.3 By virtue of s 20(3), any statutory instrument made under s 14 (designated derogations), s 15 (designated reservations) or s 16(7) (amendment of the 1998 Act following withdrawal of a designated derogation) must be laid before Parliament.

19.4 Section 20(4) provides that no order may be made by the Lord Chancellor or the Secretary of State under s 1(4) (amendments by the Secretary of State to reflect the effect of a protocol to the Convention), s 7(11) (amendments to provide tribunals with 'appropriate remedies' in relation to an unlawful act by a public authority) or s 16(2) (orders by the Secretary of State to extend the life span of a designated derogation from the Convention) unless a draft of the order has been laid before, and approved by Parliament.

19.5 Section 20(6), (7) and (8) relate to the power of a Northern Ireland department to make rules and orders under HRA 1998.

INTERPRETATION, ETC

19.6 Section 21 is the interpretation section of the 1998 Act. Section 21(1) defines 15 terms, including 'primary legislation', 'subordinate legislation', and 'tribunal'.

19.7 'Primary legislation' is defined as meaning inter alia any 'public general Act.' Lord Henley questioned whether this term included Acts of the old Parliaments, some of which remain on the statute books. In the Lord Advocate's view, the enactments of old Parliaments which preceded the UK Parliament, such as those enactments of the English and Scottish Parliaments passed before the Act of Union 1707, the Parliament of Great Britain between 1707–1801 and the Parliament of Ireland pre-1801, 'must be primary legislation for the purposes of this Bill.'[1]

---

[1]   Lord Hardie: HL Report, 29 January 1998, col 416.

19.8 It is noticeable that Orders in Council made in exercise of the Royal Prerogative are also included within the meaning of 'primary legislation' in s 21. Thus, Orders in Council are susceptible to declarations of incompatibility under s 4 of the 1998 Act, if the courts find it impossible to read and to give effect to such Orders in Council in a way which is compatible with the Convention rights.

19.9   Section 21(2)–(4) explains the references used in s 2(1) concerning the Articles of the Convention and reports and decisions of the Commission and the Committee of Ministers. They reflect that all such determinations by the Commission and the Committee of Ministers fall within the Articles of the Convention before the addition of Protocol 11. Hence, under the new system with effect from 1 November 1998 the Articles referred to in s 2(1) concerning the Commission and Committee of Ministers are absent from the Convention as amended by Protocol 11. Section 21(5) deals with the effects of the Government's acceptance to abolish the death penalty (see also para 19.15 below), stating that—

> 'Any liability under the Army Act 1955, the Air Force Act 1955 or the Naval Discipline Act 1957 to suffer death for an offence is replaced by a liability to imprisonment for life or any less punishment authorised by those Acts; and those Acts shall accordingly have effect with the necessary modifications.'.

COMMENCEMENT, APPLICATION AND EXTENT

Commencement

19.10   By virtue of s 22(2), ss 18, 20 and 21(5) came into force on the passing of the 1998 Act, ie 9 November 1998. Section 22(3) provides that the other provisions of the 1998 Act shall come into force on days to be appointed by the Secretary of State.

Application

19.11   Section 22(4) provides that s 7(1)(b) 'applies to proceedings brought by or at the instigation of a public authority whenever the act in question took place; but otherwise that subsection does not apply to an act taking place before the coming into force of that section.' This section thus seeks to distinguish between proceedings initiated under s 7(1)(a) of the 1998 Act, ie claims based solely on HRA 1998, and those initiated under s 7(1)(b), ie reliance on Convention rights in 'any legal proceedings', insofar as the retrospective application of the Act applies. However, it should be borne in mind that s 6(1), by which an act by a public authority which is incompatible with a Convention right is made 'unlawful', is also expected to take effect on the same day as s 7, namely 2 October 2000. Thus it is arguable whether, notwithstanding the provisions of s 22(4), an individual can complain that an act of a public authority which took place retrospectively, ie before 2 October 2000, was 'unlawful' under the 1998 Act, regardless as to whether his or her claim falls under either option under s 7(1).

Miscellaneous

19.12   The 1998 Act binds the Crown (s 22(5)) and it extends to Northern Ireland (s 22(6)). Section 22(7) provides that the abolition of the death penalty for military offences extends to any place in which the Armed Forces Acts apply (see para 19.9).

Appendix 1

Human Rights Act 1998

Human Rights Act 1998

(1998 c 42)

ARRANGEMENT OF SECTIONS

An Act to give further effect to rights and freedoms guaranteed under the European Convention on Human Rights; to make provision with respect to holders of certain judicial offices who become judges of the European Court of Human Rights; and for connected purposes.

[9 November 1998]

Parliamentary debates.

House of Lords:

2nd Reading 3 November 1997: 582 HL Official Report (5th series) col 1227.

Committee Stage 18 November 1997: 583 HL Official Report (5th series) cols 466, 490, 533; 24 November 1997: 583 HL Official Report (5th series) cols 754, 771, 823; 27 November 1997: 583 HL Official Report (5th series) cols 1091, 1139.

Report Stage 19 January 1998: 584 HL Official Report (5th series) cols 1252, 1317; 29 January 1998: 585 HL Official Report (5th series) col 379.

3rd Reading 5 February 1998: 585 HL Official Report (5th series) col 747.

Consideration of Commons Amendments 22 October 1998: 593 HL Official Report (5th series) col 1682; 29 October 1998: 593 HL Official Report (5th series) col 2084.

House of Commons:

2nd Reading 16 February 1998: 306 HC Official Report (6th series) col 769.

Committee Stage 20 May 1998: 312 HC Official Report (6th series) col 975; 3 June 1998: 313 HC Official Report (6th series) col 388; 17 June 1998: 314 HC Official Report (6th series) col 391; 24 June 1998: 314 HC Official Report (6th series) col 1054; 2 July 1998: 315 HC Official Report (6th series) col 534.

Report Stage 21 October 1998: 317 HC Official Report (6th series) col 1294.

3rd Reading 21 October 1998: 317 HC Official Report (6th series) col 1357.

Introduction

1 The Convention Rights

(1)   In this Act "the Convention rights" means the rights and fundamental freedoms set out in—

    (a)   Articles 2 to 12 and 14 of the Convention,

    (b)   Articles 1 to 3 of the First Protocol, and

    (c)   Articles 1 and 2 of the Sixth Protocol,

as read with Articles 16 to 18 of the Convention.

(2)   Those Articles are to have effect for the purposes of this Act subject to any designated derogation or reservation (as to which see sections 14 and 15).

(3)   The Articles are set out in Schedule 1.

(4)   The Secretary of State may by order make such amendments to this Act as he considers appropriate to reflect the effect, in relation to the United Kingdom, of a protocol.

(5)   In subsection (4) "protocol" means a protocol to the Convention—

    (a)   which the United Kingdom has ratified; or

    (b)   which the United Kingdom has signed with a view to ratification.

(6)   No amendment may be made by an order under subsection (4) so as to come into force before the protocol concerned is in force in relation to the United Kingdom.

Definitions   For "designated derogation", see s 14(1) post; for "designated reservation", see s 15(1) post; as to amendments, and for "the Convention", "the First Protocol" and "the Sixth Protocol", see s 21(1) post.
References   See paras 1.6, 1.10, 1.17; 3.1–3.5; 4.19.

2 Interpretation of Convention rights

(1)   A court or tribunal determining a question which has arisen in connection with a Convention right must take into account any—

(a)   judgment, decision, declaration or advisory opinion of the European Court of Human Rights,

(b)   opinion of the Commission given in a report adopted under Article 31 of the Convention,

(c)   decision of the Commission in connection with Article 26 or 27(2) of the Convention, or

(d)   decision of the Committee of Ministers taken under Article 46 of the Convention,

whenever made or given, so far as, in the opinion of the court or tribunal, it is relevant to the proceedings in which that question has arisen.

(2)   Evidence of any judgment, decision, declaration or opinion of which account may have to be taken under this section is to be given in proceedings before any court or tribunal in such manner as may be provided by rules.

(3)   In this section "rules" means rules of court or, in the case of proceedings before a tribunal, rules made for the purposes of this section—

(a)   by the Lord Chancellor or the Secretary of State, in relation to any proceedings outside Scotland;

(b)   by the Secretary of State, in relation to proceedings in Scotland; or

(c)   by a Northern Ireland department, in relation to proceedings before a tribunal in Northern Ireland—

(i)   which deals with transferred matters; and

(ii)   for which no rules made under paragraph (a) are in force.

Definitions   For "Convention right", see s 1(1) ante; for "the Commission", "the Convention", "transferred matters" and "tribunal", see s 21(1) post.
References   See paras 1.18, 1.19; 4.1–4.5, 4.9, 4.11, 4.25, 4.26; 10.8.

Legislation

3 Interpretation of legislation

(1)   So far as it is possible to do so, primary legislation and subordinate legislation must be read and given effect in a way which is compatible with the Convention rights.

(2)   This section—

(a)   applies to primary legislation and subordinate legislation whenever enacted;

(b)   does not affect the validity, continuing operation or enforcement of any incompatible primary legislation; and

(c)   does not affect the validity, continuing operation or enforcement of any incompatible subordinate legislation if (disregarding any possibility of revocation) primary legislation prevents removal of the incompatibility.

Definitions   For "the Convention rights", see s 1(1) ante; for "primary legislation" and "subordinate legislation", see s 22(1) post.
References   See paras 1.12, 1.13; 5.1–5.18, 10.16.

4 Declaration of incompatibility

(1) Subsection (2) applies in any proceedings in which a court determines whether a provision of primary legislation is compatible with a Convention right.

(2) If the court is satisfied that the provision is incompatible with a Convention right, it may make a declaration of that incompatibility.

(3) Subsection (4) applies in any proceedings in which a court determines whether a provision of subordinate legislation, made in the exercise of a power conferred by primary legislation, is compatible with a Convention right.

(4) If the court is satisfied—

    (a) that the provision is incompatible with a Convention right, and

    (b) that (disregarding any possibility of revocation) the primary legislation concerned prevents removal of the incompatibility,

it may make a declaration of that incompatibility.

(5) In this section "court" means—

    (a) the House of Lords;

    (b) the Judicial Committee of the Privy Council;

    (c) the Courts-Martial Appeal Court;

    (d) in Scotland, the High Court of Justiciary sitting otherwise than as a trial court or the Court of Session;

    (e) in England and Wales or Northern Ireland, the High Court or the Court of Appeal.

(6) A declaration under this section ("a declaration of incompatibility")—

    (a) does not affect the validity, continuing operation or enforcement of the provision in respect of which it is given; and

    (b) is not binding on the parties to the proceedings in which it is made.

Definitions For "Convention right", see s 1(1) ante; for "primary legislation" and "subordinate legislation", see s 21(1) post.
References See paras 1.13, 1.14; 5.7; 6.1–6.6, 6.9, 6.11, 6.12; 7.1; 19.8.

5 Right of Crown to intervene

(1) Where a court is considering whether to make a declaration of incompatibility, the Crown is entitled to notice in accordance with rules of court.

(2) In any case to which subsection (1) applies—

    (a) a Minister of the Crown (or a person nominated by him),

    (b) a member of the Scottish Executive,

    (c) a Northern Ireland Minister,

    (d) a Northern Ireland department,

is entitled, on giving notice in accordance with rules of court, to be joined as a party to the proceedings.

(3) Notice under subsection (2) may be given at any time during the proceedings.

(4) A person who has been made a party to criminal proceedings (other than in Scotland) as the result of a notice under subsection (2) may, with leave, appeal to the House of Lords against any declaration of incompatibility made in the proceedings.

(5) In subsection (4)—

    "criminal proceedings" includes all proceedings before the Courts-Martial Appeal Court; and

    "leave" means leave granted by the court making the declaration of incompatibility or by the House of Lords.

Definitions   For "declaration of incompatibility", "Minister of the Crown" and "Northern Ireland Minister", see s 21(1) post.
References   See paras 1.13; 7.1–7.6.

Public authorities

6 Acts of public authorities

(1)   It is unlawful for a public authority to act in a way which is incompatible with a Convention right.

(2)   Subsection (1) does not apply to an act if—
    (a)   as the result of one or more provisions of primary legislation, the authority could not have acted differently; or
    (b)   in the case of one or more provisions of, or made under, primary legislation which cannot be read or given effect in a way which is compatible with the Convention rights, the authority was acting so as to give effect to or enforce those provisions.

(3)   In this section "public authority" includes—
    (a)   a court or tribunal, and
    (b)   any person certain of whose functions are functions of a public nature,
but does not include either House of Parliament or a person exercising functions in connection with proceedings in Parliament.

(4)   In subsection (3) "Parliament" does not include the House of Lords in its judicial capacity.

(5)   In relation to a particular act, a person is not a public authority by virtue only of subsection (3)(b) if the nature of the act is private.

(6)   "An act" includes a failure to act but does not include a failure to—
    (a)   introduce in, or lay before, Parliament a proposal for legislation; or
    (b)   make any primary legislation or remedial order.

Definitions   For "the Convention rights", see s 1(1) ante; for "primary legislation", "remedial order" and "tribunal", see s 21(1) post.
References   See paras 1.7; 4.16; 8.1–8.5, 8.8–8.12, 8.14, 8.17–8.19; 11.2; 19.11.

7 Proceedings

(1)   A person who claims that a public authority has acted (or proposes to act) in a way which is made unlawful by section 6(1) may—
    (a)   bring proceedings against the authority under this Act in the appropriate court or tribunal, or
    (b)   rely on the Convention right or rights concerned in any legal proceedings,
but only if he is (or would be) a victim of the unlawful act.

(2)   In subsection (1)(a) "appropriate court or tribunal" means such court or tribunal as may be determined in accordance with rules; and proceedings against an authority include a counterclaim or similar proceeding.

(3)   If the proceedings are brought on an application for judicial review, the applicant is to be taken to have a sufficient interest in relation to the unlawful act only if he is, or would be, a victim of that act.

(4)   If the proceedings are made by way of a petition for judicial review in Scotland, the applicant shall be taken to have title and interest to sue in relation to the unlawful act only if he is, or would be, a victim of that act.

(5)   Proceedings under subsection (1)(a) must be brought before the end of—

    (a)   the period of one year beginning with the date on which the act complained of took place; or

    (b)   such longer period as the court or tribunal considers equitable having regard to all the circumstances,

but that is subject to any rule imposing a stricter time limit in relation to the procedure in question.

(6)   In subsection (1)(b) "legal proceedings" includes—

    (a)   proceedings brought by or at the instigation of a public authority; and

    (b)   an appeal against the decision of a court or tribunal.

(7)   For the purposes of this section, a person is a victim of an unlawful act only if he would be a victim for the purposes of Article 34 of the Convention if proceedings were brought in the European Court of Human Rights in respect of that act.

(8)   Nothing in this Act creates a criminal offence.

(9)   In this section "rules" means—

    (a)   in relation to proceedings before a court or tribunal outside Scotland, rules made by the Lord Chancellor or the Secretary of State for the purposes of this section or rules of court,

    (b)   in relation to proceedings before a court or tribunal in Scotland, rules made by the Secretary of State for those purposes,

    (c)   in relation to proceedings before a tribunal in Northern Ireland—

        (i)   which deals with transferred matters; and

        (ii)   for which no rules made under paragraph (a) are in force,

rules made by a Northern Ireland department for those purposes,

and includes provision made by order under section 1 of the Courts and Legal Services Act 1990.

(10)   In making rules, regard must be had to section 9.

(11)   The Minister who has power to make rules in relation to a particular tribunal may, to the extent he considers it necessary to ensure that the tribunal can provide an appropriate remedy in relation to an act (or proposed act) of a public authority which is (or would be) unlawful as a result of section 6(1), by order add to—

    (a)   the relief or remedies which the tribunal may grant; or

    (b)   the grounds on which it may grant any of them.

(12)   An order made under subsection (11) may contain such incidental, supplemental, consequential or transitional provision as the Minister making it considers appropriate.

(13)   "The Minister" includes the Northern Ireland department concerned.

Definitions   For "the Convention right", see s 1(1) *ante*; as to "act", see s 6(6) *ante*; for "public authority", see s 6(3) *ante*; for "the Convention", "transferred matters" and "tribunal", see s 21(1) *post*.
References   See paras 1.7, 1.22, 1.24, 1.32; 9.1–9.15, 9.20–9.23; 10.17; 19.11.

8 Judicial remedies

(1)   In relation to any act (or proposed act) of a public authority which the court finds is (or would be) unlawful, it may grant such relief or remedy, or make such order, within its powers as it considers just and appropriate.

(2)   But damages may be awarded only by a court which has power to award damages, or to order the payment of compensation, in civil proceedings.

(3)   No award of damages is to be made unless, taking account of all the circumstances of the case, including—

(a)   any other relief or remedy granted, or order made, in relation to the act in question (by that or any other court), and

(b)   the consequences of any decision (of that or any other court) in respect of that act,

the court is satisfied that the award is necessary to afford just satisfaction to the person in whose favour it is made.

(4)   In determining—

(a)   whether to award damages, or

(b)   the amount of an award,

the court must take into account the principles applied by the European Court of Human Rights in relation to the award of compensation under Article 41 of the Convention.

(5)   A public authority against which damages are awarded is to be treated—

(a)   in Scotland, for the purposes of section 3 of the Law Reform (Miscellaneous Provisions) (Scotland) Act 1940 as if the award were made in an action of damages in which the authority has been found liable in respect of loss or damage to the person to whom the award is made;

(b)   for the purposes of the Civil Liability (Contribution) Act 1978 as liable in respect of damage suffered by the person to whom the award is made.

(6)   In this section—

"court" includes a tribunal;

"damages" means damages for an unlawful act of a public authority; and

"unlawful" means unlawful under section 6(1).

Definitions   For "act", see s 6(6) ante; for "the Convention" and "tribunal", see s 21(1) post.
References   See paras 1.7, 1.27; 3.14; 10.1–10.9, 10.11–10.13, 10.19–10.21.

---

9 Judicial acts

(1)   Proceedings under section 7(1)(a) in respect of a judicial act may be brought only—

(a)   by exercising a right of appeal;

(b)   on an application (in Scotland a petition) for judicial review; or

(c)   in such other forum as may be prescribed by rules.

(2)   That does not affect any rule of law which prevents a court from being the subject of judicial review.

(3)   In proceedings under this Act in respect of a judicial act done in good faith, damages may not be awarded otherwise than to compensate a person to the extent required by Article 5(5) of the Convention.

(4)   An award of damages permitted by subsection (3) is to be made against the Crown; but no award may be made unless the appropriate person, if not a party to the proceedings, is joined.

(5)   In this section—

"appropriate person" means the Minister responsible for the court concerned, or a person or government department nominated by him;

"court" includes a tribunal;

"judge" includes a member of a tribunal, a justice of the peace and a clerk or other officer entitled to exercise the jurisdiction of a court;

"judicial act" means a judicial act of a court and includes an act done on the instructions, or on behalf, of a judge; and

"rules" has the same meaning as in section 7(9).

Definitions   For "act", see s 6(6) ante; for "rules", see, by virtue of sub-s (5) above, s 7(9) ante; for "the Convention" and "tribunal", see s 21(1) post.
References   See paras 1.7, 1.31; 11.1–11.3, 11.6–11.11.

Remedial action

10 Power to take remedial action

(1)   This section applies if—

    (a)   a provision of legislation has been declared under section 4 to be incompatible with a Convention right and, if an appeal lies—

        (i)   all persons who may appeal have stated in writing that they do not intend to do so;

        (ii)   the time for bringing an appeal has expired and no appeal has been brought within that time; or

        (iii)   an appeal brought within that time has been determined or abandoned; or

    (b)   it appears to a Minister of the Crown or Her Majesty in Council that, having regard to a finding of the European Court of Human Rights made after the coming into force of this section in proceedings against the United Kingdom, a provision of legislation is incompatible with an obligation of the United Kingdom arising from the Convention.

(2)   If a Minister of the Crown considers that there are compelling reasons for proceeding under this section, he may by order make such amendments to the legislation as he considers necessary to remove the incompatibility.

(3)   If, in the case of subordinate legislation, a Minister of the Crown considers—

    (a)   that it is necessary to amend the primary legislation under which the subordinate legislation in question was made, in order to enable the incompatibility to be removed, and

    (b)   that there are compelling reasons for proceeding under this section,

he may by order make such amendments to the primary legislation as he considers necessary.

(4)   This section also applies where the provision in question is in subordinate legislation and has been quashed, or declared invalid, by reason of incompatibility with a Convention right and the Minister proposes to proceed under paragraph 2(b) of Schedule 2.

(5)   If the legislation is an Order in Council, the power conferred by subsection (2) or (3) is exercisable by Her Majesty in Council.

(6)   In this section "legislation" does not include a Measure of the Church Assembly or of the General Synod of the Church of England.

(7)   Schedule 2 makes further provision about remedial orders.

Definitions   For "Convention right", see s 1(1) ante; for "amend", "the Convention", "Minister of the Crown", "primary legislation", "remedial order" and "subordinate legislation", see s 21(1) post.
References   See paras 1.14; 6.17; 7.5; 12.1, 12.3–12.18.

Other rights and proceedings

11 Safeguard for existing human rights

A person's reliance on a Convention right does not restrict—
(a) any other right or freedom conferred on him by or under any law having effect in any part of the United Kingdom; or
(b) his right to make any claim or bring any proceedings which he could make or bring apart from sections 7 to 9.

Definitions For "Convention right", see s 1(1) ante.
References See paras 13.1–13.3.

---

12 Freedom of expression

(1) This section applies if a court is considering whether to grant any relief which, if granted, might affect the exercise of the Convention right to freedom of expression.

(2) If the person against whom the application for relief is made ("the respondent") is neither present nor represented, no such relief is to be granted unless the court is satisfied—
(a) that the applicant has taken all practicable steps to notify the respondent; or
(b) that there are compelling reasons why the respondent should not be notified.

(3) No such relief is to be granted so as to restrain publication before trial unless the court is satisfied that the applicant is likely to establish that publication should not be allowed.

(4) The court must have particular regard to the importance of the Convention right to freedom of expression and, where the proceedings relate to material which the respondent claims, or which appears to the court, to be journalistic, literary or artistic material (or to conduct connected with such material), to—
(a) the extent to which—
(i) the material has, or is about to, become available to the public; or
(ii) it is, or would be, in the public interest for the material to be published;
(b) any relevant privacy code.

(5) In this section—
"court" includes a tribunal; and
"relief" includes any remedy or order (other than in criminal proceedings).

Definitions For "Convention right", see s 1(1) ante; for "the Convention" and "tribunal", see s 21(1) post.
References See paras 14.1–14.11.

---

13 Freedom of thought, conscience and religion

(1) If a court's determination of any question arising under this Act might affect the exercise by a religious organisation (itself or its members collectively) of the Convention right to freedom of thought, conscience and religion, it must have particular regard to the importance of that right.

(2) In this section "court" includes a tribunal.

Definitions For "Convention right", see s 1(1) ante; for "the Convention" and "tribunal", see s 21(1) post.
References See paras 15.1–15.5

Derogations and reservations

14 Derogations

(1)   In this Act "designated derogation" means—

    (a)   the United Kingdom's derogation from Article 5(3) of the Convention; and

    (b)   any derogation by the United Kingdom from an Article of the Convention, or of any protocol to the Convention, which is designated for the purposes of this Act in an order made by the Secretary of State.

(2)   The derogation referred to in subsection (1)(a) is set out in Part I of Schedule 3.

(3)   If a designated derogation is amended or replaced it ceases to be a designated derogation.

(4)   But subsection (3) does not prevent the Secretary of State from exercising his power under subsection (1)(b) to make a fresh designation order in respect of the Article concerned.

(5)   The Secretary of State must by order make such amendments to Schedule 3 as he considers appropriate to reflect—

    (a)   any designation order; or

    (b)   the effect of subsection (3).

(6)   A designation order may be made in anticipation of the making by the United Kingdom of a proposed derogation.

Definitions   As to amendments and amending, and for "the Convention", see s 21(1) post.
References   See paras 3.4; 16.1–16.3, 16.6, 16.9.

15 Reservations

(1)   In this Act "designated reservation" means—

    (a)   the United Kingdom's reservation to Article 2 of the First Protocol to the Convention; and

    (b)   any other reservation by the United Kingdom to an Article of the Convention, or of any protocol to the Convention, which is designated for the purposes of this Act in an order made by the Secretary of State.

(2)   The text of the reservation referred to in subsection (1)(a) is set out in Part II of Schedule 3.

(3)   If a designated reservation is withdrawn wholly or in part it ceases to be a designated reservation.

(4)   But subsection (3) does not prevent the Secretary of State from exercising his power under subsection (1)(b) to make a fresh designation order in respect of the Article concerned.

(5)   The Secretary of State must by order make such amendments to this Act as he considers appropriate to reflect—

    (a)   any designation order; or

    (b)   the effect of subsection (3).

Definitions   As to amendments, and for "the Convention" and "the First Protocol", see s 21(1) post.
References   See paras 3.4; 16.1–16.4, 16.9.

16 Period for which designated derogations have effect

(1)   If it has not already been withdrawn by the United Kingdom, a designated derogation ceases to have effect for the purposes of this Act—

    (a)   in the case of the derogation referred to in section 14(1)(a), at the end of the period of five years beginning with the date on which section 1(2) came into force;

    (b)   in the case of any other derogation, at the end of the period of five years beginning with the date on which the order designating it was made.

(2)   At any time before the period—

    (a)   fixed by subsection (1)(a) or (b), or

    (b)   extended by an order under this subsection,

comes to an end, the Secretary of State may by order extend it by a further period of five years.

(3)   An order under section 14(1)(b) ceases to have effect at the end of the period for consideration, unless a resolution has been passed by each House approving the order.

(4)   Subsection (3) does not affect—

    (a)   anything done in reliance on the order; or

    (b)   the power to make a fresh order under section 14(1)(b).

(5)   In subsection (3) "period for consideration" means the period of forty days beginning with the day on which the order was made.

(6)   In calculating the period for consideration, no account is to be taken of any time during which—

    (a)   Parliament is dissolved or prorogued; or

    (b)   both Houses are adjourned for more than four days.

(7)   If a designated derogation is withdrawn by the United Kingdom, the Secretary of State must by order make such amendments to this Act as he considers are required to reflect that withdrawal.

Definitions   As to amendments, and for "designated derogation", see s 14(1) ante.
References   See paras 16.2, 16.6, 16.7, 16.9; 19.4.

17 Periodic review of designated reservations

(1)   The appropriate Minister must review the designated reservation referred to in section 15(1)(a)—

    (a)   before the end of the period of five years beginning with the date on which section 1(2) came into force; and

    (b)   if that designation is still in force, before the end of the period of five years beginning with the date on which the last report relating to it was laid under subsection (3).

(2)   The appropriate Minister must review each of the other designated reservations (if any)—

    (a)   before the end of the period of five years beginning with the date on which the order designating the reservation first came into force; and

    (b)   if the designation is still in force, before the end of the period of five years beginning with the date on which the last report relating to it was laid under subsection (3).

(3)   The Minister conducting a review under this section must prepare a report on the result of the review and lay a copy of it before each House of Parliament.

Definitions For "designated reservation", see s 15(1) ante; for "the appropriate Minister" see s 21(1) post.
References See paras 3.4; 16.2, 16.7.

Judges of the European Court of Human Rights

18 Appointment to European Court of Human Rights

(1)   In this section "judicial office" means the office of—

    (a)   Lord Justice of Appeal, Justice of the High Court or Circuit judge, in England and Wales;

    (b)   judge of the Court of Session or sheriff, in Scotland;

    (c)   Lord Justice of Appeal, judge of the High Court or county court judge, in Northern Ireland.

(2)   The holder of a judicial office may become a judge of the European Court of Human Rights ("the Court") without being required to relinquish his office.

(3)   But he is not required to perform the duties of his judicial office while he is a judge of the Court.

(4)   In respect of any period during which he is a judge of the Court—

    (a)   a Lord Justice of Appeal or Justice of the High Court is not to count as a judge of the relevant court for the purposes of section 2(1) or 4(1) of the Supreme Court Act 1981 (maximum number of judges) nor as a judge of the Supreme Court for the purposes of section 12(1) to (6) of that Act (salaries etc);

    (b)   a judge of the Court of Session is not to count as a judge of that court for the purposes of section 1(1) of the Court of Session Act 1988 (maximum number of judges) or of section 9(1)(c) of the Administration of Justice Act 1973 ("the 1973 Act") (salaries etc);

    (c)   a Lord Justice of Appeal or judge of the High Court in Northern Ireland is not to count as a judge of the relevant court for the purposes of section 2(1) or 3(1) of the Judicature (Northern Ireland) Act 1978 (maximum number of judges) nor as a judge of the Supreme Court of Northern Ireland for the purposes of section 9(1)(d) of the 1973 Act (salaries etc);

    (d)   a Circuit judge is not to count as such for the purposes of section 18 of the Courts Act 1971 (salaries etc);

    (e)   a sheriff is not to count as such for the purposes of section 14 of the Sheriff Courts (Scotland) Act 1907 (salaries etc);

    (f)   a county court judge of Northern Ireland is not to count as such for the purposes of section 106 of the County Courts Act (Northern Ireland) 1959 (salaries etc).

(5)   If a sheriff principal is appointed a judge of the Court, section 11(1) of the Sheriff Courts (Scotland) Act 1971 (temporary appointment of sheriff principal) applies, while he holds that appointment, as if his office is vacant.

(6)   Schedule 4 makes provision about judicial pensions in relation to the holder of a judicial office who serves as a judge of the Court.

(7)   The Lord Chancellor or the Secretary of State may by order make such transitional provision (including, in particular, provision for a temporary increase in the maximum number of judges) as he considers appropriate in relation to any holder of a judicial office who has completed his service as a judge of the Court.

References See paras 17.2–17.6, 17.10.

Parliamentary procedure

19 Statements of compatibility

(1)   A Minister of the Crown in charge of a Bill in either House of Parliament must, before Second Reading of the Bill—

    (a)   make a statement to the effect that in his view the provisions of the Bill are compatible with the Convention rights ("a statement of compatibility"); or

    (b)   make a statement to the effect that although he is unable to make a statement of compatibility the government nevertheless wishes the House to proceed with the Bill.

(2)   The statement must be in writing and be published in such manner as the Minister making it considers appropriate.

Definitions   For "the Convention rights", see s 1(1) ante; for "the Convention" and "Minister of the Crown", see s 21(1) post.
References   See paras 1.11; 18.1–18.5, 18.7.

Supplemental

20 Orders etc under this Act

(1)   Any power of a Minister of the Crown to make an order under this Act is exercisable by statutory instrument.

(2)   The power of the Lord Chancellor or the Secretary of State to make rules (other than rules of court) under section 2(3) or 7(9) is exercisable by statutory instrument.

(3)   Any statutory instrument made under section 14, 15 or 16(7) must be laid before Parliament.

(4)   No order may be made by the Lord Chancellor or the Secretary of State under section 1(4), 7(11) or 16(2) unless a draft of the order has been laid before, and approved by, each House of Parliament.

(5)   Any statutory instrument made under section 18(7) or Schedule 4, or to which subsection (2) applies, shall be subject to annulment in pursuance of a resolution of either House of Parliament.

(6)   The power of a Northern Ireland department to make—

    (a)   rules under section 2(3)(c) or 7(9)(c), or

    (b)   an order under section 7(11),

is exercisable by statutory rule for the purposes of the Statutory Rules (Northern Ireland) Order 1979.

(7)   Any rules made under section 2(3)(c) or 7(9)(c) shall be subject to negative resolution; and section 41(6) of the Interpretation Act (Northern Ireland) 1954 (meaning of "subject to negative resolution") shall apply as if the power to make the rules were conferred by an Act of the Northern Ireland Assembly.

(8)   No order may be made by a Northern Ireland department under section 7(11) unless a draft of the order has been laid before, and approved by, the Northern Ireland Assembly.

Definitions   For "Minister of the Crown", see s 21(1) post.
References   See paras 19.1–19.5.

---

21 Interpretation, etc

(1)   In this Act—
"amend" includes repeal and apply (with or without modifications);
"the appropriate Minister" means the Minister of the Crown having charge
    of the appropriate authorised government department (within the
    meaning of the Crown Proceedings Act 1947);
"the Commission" means the European Commission of Human Rights;
"the Convention" means the Convention for the Protection of Human
    Rights and Fundamental Freedoms, agreed by the Council of Europe
    at Rome on 4th November 1950 as it has effect for the time being in
    relation to the United Kingdom;
"declaration of incompatibility" means a declaration under section 4;
"Minister of the Crown" has the same meaning as in the Ministers of the
    Crown Act 1975;
"Northern Ireland Minister" includes the First Minister and the deputy
    First Minister in Northern Ireland;
"primary legislation" means any—
    (a)   public general Act;
    (b)   local and personal Act;
    (c)   private Act;
    (d)   Measure of the Church Assembly;
    (e)   Measure of the General Synod of the Church of England;
    (f)   Order in Council—
        (i)   made in exercise of Her Majesty's Royal Prerogative;
        (ii)   made under section 38(1)(a) of the Northern Ireland
           Constitution Act 1973 or the corresponding provision of the
           Northern Ireland Act 1998; or
        (iii) amending an Act of a kind mentioned in paragraph (a), (b)
           or (c);
and includes an order or other instrument made under primary legislation
(otherwise than by the National Assembly for Wales, a member of the
Scottish Executive, a Northern Ireland Minister or a Northern Ireland
department) to the extent to which it operates to bring one or more
provisions of that legislation into force or amends any primary legislation;
"the First Protocol" means the protocol to the Convention agreed at Paris
    on 20th March 1952;
"the Sixth Protocol" means the protocol to the Convention agreed at
    Strasbourg on 28th April 1983;
"the Eleventh Protocol" means the protocol to the Convention
    (restructuring the control machinery established by the Convention)
    agreed at Strasbourg on 11th May 1994;
"remedial order" means an order under section 10;
"subordinate legislation" means any—
    (a)   Order in Council other than one—
        (i)   made in exercise of Her Majesty's Royal Prerogative;
        (ii)   made under section 38(1)(a) of the Northern Ireland
           Constitution Act 1973 or the corresponding provision of the
           Northern Ireland Act 1998; or
        (iii) amending an Act of a kind mentioned in the definition of
           primary legislation;
    (b)   Act of the Scottish Parliament;
    (c)   Act of the Parliament of Northern Ireland;
    (d)   Measure of the Assembly established under section 1 of the
        Northern Ireland Assembly Act 1973;
    (e)   Act of the Northern Ireland Assembly;

(f) order, rules, regulations, scheme, warrant, byelaw or other instrument made under primary legislation (except to the extent to which it operates to bring one or more provisions of that legislation into force or amends any primary legislation);

(g) order, rules, regulations, scheme, warrant, byelaw or other instrument made under legislation mentioned in paragraph (b), (c), (d) or (e) or made under an Order in Council applying only to Northern Ireland;

(h) order, rules, regulations, scheme, warrant, byelaw or other instrument made by a member of the Scottish Executive, a Northern Ireland Minister or a Northern Ireland department in exercise of prerogative or other executive functions of Her Majesty which are exercisable by such a person on behalf of Her Majesty;

"transferred matters" has the same meaning as in the Northern Ireland Act 1998; and

"tribunal" means any tribunal in which legal proceedings may be brought.

(2) The references in paragraphs (b) and (c) of section 2(1) to Articles are to Articles of the Convention as they had effect immediately before the coming into force of the Eleventh Protocol.

(3) The reference in paragraph (d) of section 2(1) to Article 46 includes a reference to Articles 32 and 54 of the Convention as they had effect immediately before the coming into force of the Eleventh Protocol.

(4) The references in section 2(1) to a report or decision of the Commission or a decision of the Committee of Ministers include references to a report or decision made as provided by paragraphs 3, 4 and 6 of Article 5 of the Eleventh Protocol (transitional provisions).

(5) Any liability under the Army Act 1955, the Air Force Act 1955 or the Naval Discipline Act 1957 to suffer death for an offence is replaced by a liability to imprisonment for life or any less punishment authorised by those Acts; and those Acts shall accordingly have effect with the necessary modifications.

References   See paras 3.10; 19.6, 19.8–19.10.

22 Short title, commencement, application and extent

(1) This Act may be cited as the Human Rights Act 1998.

(2) Sections 18, 20 and 21(5) and this section come into force on the passing of this Act.

(3) The other provisions of this Act come into force on such day as the Secretary of State may by order appoint; and different days may be appointed for different purposes.

(4) Paragraph (b) of subsection (1) of section 7 applies to proceedings brought by or at the instigation of a public authority whenever the act in question took place; but otherwise that subsection does not apply to an act taking place before the coming into force of that section.

(5) This Act binds the Crown.

(6) This Act extends to Northern Ireland.

(7) Section 21(5), so far as it relates to any provision contained in the Army Act 1955, the Air Force Act 1955 or the Naval Discipline Act 1957, extends to any place to which that provision extends.

Definitions   For "act", see s 6(6) ante.
References   See paras 19.10–19.12.

SCHEDULE 1

THE ARTICLES

PART I

THE CONVENTION

RIGHTS AND FREEDOMS

Article 2
Right to life

1.   Everyone's right to life shall be protected by law. No one shall be deprived of his life intentionally save in the execution of a sentence of a court following his conviction of a crime for which this penalty is provided by law.

2.   Deprivation of life shall not be regarded as inflicted in contravention of this Article when it results from the use of force which is no more than absolutely necessary:
   (a)   in defence of any person from unlawful violence;
   (b)   in order to effect a lawful arrest or to prevent the escape of a person lawfully detained;
   (c)   in action lawfully taken for the purpose of quelling a riot or insurrection.

Article 3
Prohibition of torture

No one shall be subjected to torture or to inhuman or degrading treatment or punishment.

Article 4
Prohibition of slavery and forced labour

1.   No one shall be held in slavery or servitude.

2.   No one shall be required to perform forced or compulsory labour.

3.   For the purpose of this Article the term "forced or compulsory labour" shall not include:
   (a)   any work required to be done in the ordinary course of detention imposed according to the provisions of Article 5 of this Convention or during conditional release from such detention;
   (b)   any service of a military character or, in case of conscientious objectors in countries where they are recognised, service exacted instead of compulsory military service;
   (c)   any service exacted in case of an emergency or calamity threatening the life or well-being of the community;
   (d)   any work or service which forms part of normal civic obligations.

Article 5
Right to liberty and security

1.   Everyone has the right to liberty and security of person. No one shall be deprived of his liberty save in the following cases and in accordance with a procedure prescribed by law:
   (a)   the lawful detention of a person after conviction by a competent court;
   (b)   the lawful arrest or detention of a person for non-compliance with the lawful order of a court or in order to secure the fulfilment of any obligation prescribed by law;
   (c)   the lawful arrest or detention of a person effected for the purpose of bringing him before the competent legal authority on reasonable suspicion of having committed an offence or when it is reasonably considered necessary to prevent his committing an offence or fleeing after having done so;
   (d)   the detention of a minor by lawful order for the purpose of educational supervision or his lawful detention for the purpose of bringing him before the competent legal authority;

(e) the lawful detention of persons for the prevention of the spreading of infectious diseases, of persons of unsound mind, alcoholics or drug addicts or vagrants;

(f) the lawful arrest or detention of a person to prevent his effecting an unauthorised entry into the country or of a person against whom action is being taken with a view to deportation or extradition.

2. Everyone who is arrested shall be informed promptly, in a language which he understands, of the reasons for his arrest and of any charge against him.

3. Everyone arrested or detained in accordance with the provisions of paragraph 1(c) of this Article shall be brought promptly before a judge or other officer authorised by law to exercise judicial power and shall be entitled to trial within a reasonable time or to release pending trial. Release may be conditioned by guarantees to appear for trial.

4. Everyone who is deprived of his liberty by arrest or detention shall be entitled to take proceedings by which the lawfulness of his detention shall be decided speedily by a court and his release ordered if the detention is not lawful.

5. Everyone who has been the victim of arrest or detention in contravention of the provisions of this Article shall have an enforceable right to compensation.

Article 6
Right to a fair trial

1. In the determination of his civil rights and obligations or of any criminal charge against him, everyone is entitled to a fair and public hearing within a reasonable time by an independent and impartial tribunal established by law. Judgment shall be pronounced publicly but the press and public may be excluded from all or part of the trial in the interest of morals, public order or national security in a democratic society, where the interests of juveniles or the protection of the private life of the parties so require, or to the extent strictly necessary in the opinion of the court in special circumstances where publicity would prejudice the interests of justice.

2. Everyone charged with a criminal offence shall be presumed innocent until proved guilty according to law.

3. Everyone charged with a criminal offence has the following minimum rights:

(a) to be informed promptly, in a language which he understands and in detail, of the nature and cause of the accusation against him;

(b) to have adequate time and facilities for the preparation of his defence;

(c) to defend himself in person or through legal assistance of his own choosing or, if he has not sufficient means to pay for legal assistance, to be given it free when the interests of justice so require;

(d) to examine or have examined witnesses against him and to obtain the attendance and examination of witnesses on his behalf under the same conditions as witnesses against him;

(e) to have the free assistance of an interpreter if he cannot understand or speak the language used in court.

Article 7
No punishment without law

1. No one shall be held guilty of any criminal offence on account of any act or omission which did not constitute a criminal offence under national or international law at the time when it was committed. Nor shall a heavier penalty be imposed than the one that was applicable at the time the criminal offence was committed.

2. This Article shall not prejudice the trial and punishment of any person for any act or omission which, at the time when it was committed, was criminal according to the general principles of law recognised by civilised nations.

Article 8
Right to respect for private and family life

1. Everyone has the right to respect for his private and family life, his home and his correspondence.

2. There shall be no interference by a public authority with the exercise of this right except such as is in accordance with the law and is necessary in a democratic society in the

interests of national security, public safety or the economic well-being of the country, for the prevention of disorder or crime, for the protection of health or morals, or for the protection of the rights and freedoms of others.

Article 9
Freedom of thought, conscience and religion

1. Everyone has the right to freedom of thought, conscience and religion; this right includes freedom to change his religion or belief and freedom, either alone or in community with others and in public or private, to manifest his religion or belief, in worship, teaching, practice and observance.

2. Freedom to manifest one's religion or beliefs shall be subject only to such limitations as are prescribed by law and are necessary in a democratic society in the interests of public safety, for the protection of public order, health or morals, or for the protection of the rights and freedoms of others.

Article 10
Freedom of expression

1. Everyone has the right to freedom of expression. This right shall include freedom to hold opinions and to receive and impart information and ideas without interference by public authority and regardless of frontiers. This Article shall not prevent States from requiring the licensing of broadcasting, television or cinema enterprises.

2. The exercise of these freedoms, since it carries with it duties and responsibilities, may be subject to such formalities, conditions, restrictions or penalties as are prescribed by law and are necessary in a democratic society, in the interests of national security, territorial integrity or public safety, for the prevention of disorder or crime, for the protection of health or morals, for the protection of the reputation or rights of others, for preventing the disclosure of information received in confidence, or for maintaining the authority and impartiality of the judiciary.

Article 11
Freedom of assembly and association

1. Everyone has the right to freedom of peaceful assembly and to freedom of association with others, including the right to form and to join trade unions for the protection of his interests.

2. No restrictions shall be placed on the exercise of these rights other than such as are prescribed by law and are necessary in a democratic society in the interests of national security or public safety, for the prevention of disorder or crime, for the protection of health or morals or for the protection of the rights and freedoms of others. This Article shall not prevent the imposition of lawful restrictions on the exercise of these rights by members of the armed forces, of the police or of the administration of the State.

Article 12
Right to marry

Men and women of marriageable age have the right to marry and to found a family, according to the national laws governing the exercise of this right.

Article 14
Prohibition of discrimination

The enjoyment of the rights and freedoms set forth in this Convention shall be secured without discrimination on any ground such as sex, race, colour, language, religion, political or other opinion, national or social origin, association with a national minority, property, birth or other status.

Article 16
Restrictions on political activity of aliens

Nothing in Articles 10, 11 and 14 shall be regarded as preventing the High Contracting Parties from imposing restrictions on the political activity of aliens.

Article 17
Prohibition of abuse of rights

Nothing in this Convention may be interpreted as implying for any State, group or person any right to engage in any activity or perform any act aimed at the destruction of any of the rights and freedoms set forth herein or at their limitation to a greater extent than is provided for in the Convention.

Article 18
Limitation on use of restrictions on rights

The restrictions permitted under this Convention to the said rights and freedoms shall not be applied for any purpose other than those for which they have been prescribed.

Definitions For "the Convention", see s 21(1) ante.
References See paras 3.1, 3.3.

PART II

THE FIRST PROTOCOL

Article 1
Protection of property

Every natural or legal person is entitled to the peaceful enjoyment of his possessions. No one shall be deprived of his possessions except in the public interest and subject to the conditions provided for by law and by the general principles of international law.

The preceding provisions shall not, however, in any way impair the right of a State to enforce such laws as it deems necessary to control the use of property in accordance with the general interest or to secure the payment of taxes or other contributions or penalties.

Article 2
Right to education

No person shall be denied the right to education. In the exercise of any functions which it assumes in relation to education and to teaching, the State shall respect the right of parents to ensure such education and teaching in conformity with their own religious and philosophical convictions.

Article 3
Right to free elections

The High Contracting Parties undertake to hold free elections at reasonable intervals by secret ballot, under conditions which will ensure the free expression of the opinion of the people in the choice of the legislature.

Definitions For "the First Protocol", see s 21(1) ante.
References See para 3.2.

PART III

THE SIXTH PROTOCOL

Article 1
Abolition of the death penalty

The death penalty shall be abolished. No one shall be condemned to such penalty or executed.

Article 2
Death penalty in time of war

A State may make provision in its law for the death penalty in respect of acts committed in time of war or of imminent threat of war; such penalty shall be applied only in the instances laid down in the law and in accordance with its provisions. The State shall communicate to the Secretary General of the Council of Europe the relevant provisions of that law.

Definitions For "the Sixth Protocol", see s 21(1) ante.
References See para 3.2

SCHEDULE 2

Section 10

REMEDIAL ORDERS

Orders

1.—(1) A remedial order may—

    (a)   contain such incidental, supplemental, consequential or transitional provision as the person making it considers appropriate;

    (b)   be made so as to have effect from a date earlier than that on which it is made;

    (c)   make provision for the delegation of specific functions;

    (d)   make different provision for different cases.

(2) The power conferred by sub-paragraph (1)(a) includes—

    (a)   power to amend primary legislation (including primary legislation other than that which contains the incompatible provision); and

    (b)   power to amend or revoke subordinate legislation (including subordinate legislation other than that which contains the incompatible provision).

(3) A remedial order may be made so as to have the same extent as the legislation which it affects.

(4) No person is to be guilty of an offence solely as a result of the retrospective effect of a remedial order.

Procedure

2. No remedial order may be made unless—

    (a)   a draft of the order has been approved by a resolution of each House of Parliament made after the end of the period of 60 days beginning with the day on which the draft was laid; or

    (b)   it is declared in the order that it appears to the person making it that, because of the urgency of the matter, it is necessary to make the order without a draft being so approved.

Orders laid in draft

3.—(1) No draft may be laid under paragraph 2(a) unless—

    (a)   the person proposing to make the order has laid before Parliament a document which contains a draft of the proposed order and the required information; and

    (b)   the period of 60 days, beginning with the day on which the document required by this sub-paragraph was laid, has ended.

(2) If representations have been made during that period, the draft laid under paragraph 2(a) must be accompanied by a statement containing—

    (a)   a summary of the representations; and

    (b)   if, as a result of the representations, the proposed order has been changed, details of the changes.

Urgent cases

4.—(1) If a remedial order ("the original order") is made without being approved in draft, the person making it must lay it before Parliament, accompanied by the required information, after it is made.

(2) If representations have been made during the period of 60 days beginning with the day on which the original order was made, the person making it must (after the end of that period) lay before Parliament a statement containing—

    (a)   a summary of the representations; and

    (b)   if, as a result of the representations, he considers it appropriate to make changes to the original order, details of the changes.

(3) If sub-paragraph (2)(b) applies, the person making the statement must—

    (a)   make a further remedial order replacing the original order; and

    (b)   lay the replacement order before Parliament.

(4) If, at the end of the period of 120 days beginning with the day on which the original order was made, a resolution has not been passed by each House approving the original or

replacement order, the order ceases to have effect (but without that affecting anything previously done under either order or the power to make a fresh remedial order).

Definitions

5.   In this Schedule—

   "representations" means representations about a remedial order (or proposed remedial order) made to the person making (or proposing to make) it and includes any relevant Parliamentary report or resolution; and

   "required information" means—

   (a)   an explanation of the incompatibility which the order (or proposed order) seeks to remove, including particulars of the relevant declaration, finding or order; and

   (b)   a statement of the reasons for proceeding under section 10 and for making an order in those terms.

Calculating periods

6.   In calculating any period for the purposes of this Schedule, no account is to be taken of any time during which—

   (a)   Parliament is dissolved or prorogued; or

   (b)   both Houses are adjourned for more than four days.

Definitions   For "amend", "primary legislation", "remedial order" and "subordinate legislation", see
s 21(1) ante.
References   See paras 1.14; 6.17; 7.5; 12.1, 12.19–12.31.

SCHEDULE 3

Sections 14 and 15

DEROGATION AND RESERVATION

PART I

DEROGATION

The 1988 notification

The United Kingdom Permanent Representative to the Council of Europe presents his compliments to the Secretary General of the Council, and has the honour to convey the following information in order to ensure compliance with the obligations of Her Majesty's Government in the United Kingdom under Article 15(3) of the Convention for the Protection of Human Rights and Fundamental Freedoms signed at Rome on 4 November 1950.

There have been in the United Kingdom in recent years campaigns of organised terrorism connected with the affairs of Northern Ireland which have manifested themselves in activities which have included repeated murder, attempted murder, maiming, intimidation and violent civil disturbance and in bombing and fire raising which have resulted in death, injury and widespread destruction of property. As a result, a public emergency within the meaning of Article 15(1) of the Convention exists in the United Kingdom.

The Government found it necessary in 1974 to introduce and since then, in cases concerning persons reasonably suspected of involvement in terrorism connected with the affairs of Northern Ireland, or of certain offences under the legislation, who have been detained for 48 hours, to exercise powers enabling further detention without charge, for periods of up to five days, on the authority of the Secretary of State. These powers are at present to be found in Section 12 of the Prevention of Terrorism (Temporary Provisions) Act 1984, Article 9 of the Prevention of Terrorism (Supplemental Temporary Provisions) Order 1984 and Article 10 of the Prevention of Terrorism (Supplemental Temporary Provisions) (Northern Ireland) Order 1984.

Section 12 of the Prevention of Terrorism (Temporary Provisions) Act 1984 provides for a person whom a constable has arrested on reasonable grounds of suspecting him to be guilty of an offence under Section 1, 9 or 10 of the Act, or to be or to have been involved in terrorism connected with the affairs of Northern Ireland, to be detained in right of the arrest for up to

48 hours and thereafter, where the Secretary of State extends the detention period, for up to a further five days. Section 12 substantially re-enacted Section 12 of the Prevention of Terrorism (Temporary Provisions) Act 1976 which, in turn, substantially re-enacted Section 7 of the Prevention of Terrorism (Temporary Provisions) Act 1974.

Article 10 of the Prevention of Terrorism (Supplemental Temporary Provisions) (Northern Ireland) Order 1984 (SI 1984/417) and Article 9 of the Prevention of Terrorism (Supplemental Temporary Provisions) Order 1984 (SI 1984/418) were both made under Sections 13 and 14 of and Schedule 3 to the 1984 Act and substantially re-enacted powers of detention in Orders made under the 1974 and 1976 Acts. A person who is being examined under Article 4 of either Order on his arrival in, or on seeking to leave, Northern Ireland or Great Britain for the purpose of determining whether he is or has been involved in terrorism connected with the affairs of Northern Ireland, or whether there are grounds for suspecting that he has committed an offence under Section 9 of the 1984 Act, may be detained under Article 9 or 10, as appropriate, pending the conclusion of his examination. The period of this examination may exceed 12 hours if an examining officer has reasonable grounds for suspecting him to be or to have been involved in acts of terrorism connected with the affairs of Northern Ireland.

Where such a person is detained under the said Article 9 or 10 he may be detained for up to 48 hours on the authority of an examining officer and thereafter, where the Secretary of State extends the detention period, for up to a further five days.

In its judgment of 29 November 1988 in the Case of *Brogan and Others*, the European Court of Human Rights held that there had been a violation of Article 5(3) in respect of each of the applicants, all of whom had been detained under Section 12 of the 1984 Act. The Court held that even the shortest of the four periods of detention concerned, namely four days and six hours, fell outside the constraints as to time permitted by the first part of Article 5(3). In addition, the Court held that there had been a violation of Article 5(5) in the case of each applicant.

Following this judgment, the Secretary of State for the Home Department informed Parliament on 6 December 1988 that, against the background of the terrorist campaign, and the over-riding need to bring terrorists to justice, the Government did not believe that the maximum period of detention should be reduced. He informed Parliament that the Government were examining the matter with a view to responding to the judgment. On 22 December 1988, the Secretary of State further informed Parliament that it remained the Government's wish, if it could be achieved, to find a judicial process under which extended detention might be reviewed and where appropriate authorised by a judge or other judicial officer. But a further period of reflection and consultation was necessary before the Government could bring forward a firm and final view.

Since the judgment of 29 November 1988 as well as previously, the Government have found it necessary to continue to exercise, in relation to terrorism connected with the affairs of Northern Ireland, the powers described above enabling further detention without charge for periods of up to 5 days, on the authority of the Secretary of State, to the extent strictly required by the exigencies of the situation to enable necessary enquiries and investigations properly to be completed in order to decide whether criminal proceedings should be instituted. To the extent that the exercise of these powers may be inconsistent with the obligations imposed by the Convention the Government has availed itself of the right of derogation conferred by Article 15(1) of the Convention and will continue to do so until further notice.

Dated 23 December 1988.

The 1989 notification

The United Kingdom Permanent Representative to the Council of Europe presents his compliments to the Secretary General of the Council, and has the honour to convey the following information.

In his communication to the Secretary General of 23 December 1988, reference was made to the introduction and exercise of certain powers under section 12 of the Prevention of Terrorism (Temporary Provisions) Act 1984, Article 9 of the Prevention of Terrorism (Supplemental Temporary Provisions) Order 1984 and Article 10 of the Prevention of Terrorism (Supplemental Temporary Provisions) (Northern Ireland) Order 1984.

These provisions have been replaced by section 14 of and paragraph 6 of Schedule 5 to the Prevention of Terrorism (Temporary Provisions) Act 1989, which make comparable provision. They came into force on 22 March 1989. A copy of these provisions is enclosed.

The United Kingdom Permanent Representative avails himself of this opportunity to renew to the Secretary General the assurance of his highest consideration.

23 March 1989.

Definitions   For "the Convention", see s 21(1) ante.
References   See paras 3.4; 16.1.

PART II

RESERVATION

At the time of signing the present (First) Protocol, I declare that, in view of certain provisions of the Education Acts in the United Kingdom, the principle affirmed in the second sentence of Article 2 is accepted by the United Kingdom only so far as it is compatible with the provision of efficient instruction and training, and the avoidance of unreasonable public expenditure.

Dated 20 March 1952. Made by the United Kingdom Permanent Representative to the Council of Europe.

Definitions   For "the First Protocol", see s 21(1) ante
References   See paras 3.4; 16.1, 16.4.

SCHEDULE 4

Section 18(6)

JUDICIAL PENSIONS

Duty to make orders about pensions

1.—(1) The appropriate Minister must by order make provision with respect to pensions payable to or in respect of any holder of a judicial office who serves as an ECHR judge.

(2) A pensions order must include such provision as the Minister making it considers is necessary to secure that—

    (a) an ECHR judge who was, immediately before his appointment as an ECHR judge, a member of a judicial pension scheme is entitled to remain as a member of that scheme;

    (b) the terms on which he remains a member of the scheme are those which would have been applicable had he not been appointed as an ECHR judge; and

    (c) entitlement to benefits payable in accordance with the scheme continues to be determined as if, while serving as an ECHR judge, his salary was that which would (but for section 18(4)) have been payable to him in respect of his continuing service as the holder of his judicial office.

Contributions

2. A pensions order may, in particular, make provision—

    (a) for any contributions which are payable by a person who remains a member of a scheme as a result of the order, and which would otherwise be payable by deduction from his salary, to be made otherwise than by deduction from his salary as an ECHR judge; and

    (b) for such contributions to be collected in such manner as may be determined by the administrators of the scheme.

Amendments of other enactments

3. A pensions order may amend any provision of, or made under, a pensions Act in such manner and to such extent as the Minister making the order considers necessary or expedient to ensure the proper administration of any scheme to which it relates.

Definitions

4. In this Schedule—
"appropriate Minister" means—
(a)   in relation to any judicial office whose jurisdiction is exercisable exclusively in relation to Scotland, the Secretary of State; and
(b)   otherwise, the Lord Chancellor;
"ECHR judge" means the holder of a judicial office who is serving as a judge of the Court;
"judicial pension scheme" means a scheme established by and in accordance with a pensions Act;
"pensions Act" means—
(a)   the County Courts Act (Northern Ireland) 1959;
(b)   the Sheriffs' Pensions (Scotland) Act 1961;
(c)   the Judicial Pensions Act 1981; or
(d)   the Judicial Pensions and Retirement Act 1993; and
"pensions order" means an order made under paragraph 1.

Definitions   For "judicial office", see s 18(1) ante; for "the Court", s 18(2) ante; for "the appropriate Minister" and "amend", see s 21(1) ante.
References   See paras 17.6–17.9; 19.2.

Appendix 2

Convention for the
Protection of Human Rights and
Fundamental Freedoms

Convention for the Protection of Human Rights and Fundamental Freedoms[1]

Rome, 4.XI.1950

The governments signatory hereto, being members of the Council of Europe;

Considering the Universal Declaration of Human Rights proclaimed by the General Assembly of the United Nations on 10th December 1948;

Considering that this Declaration aims at securing the universal and effective recognition and observance of the Rights therein declared;

Considering that the aim of the Council of Europe is the achievement of greater unity between its members and that one of the methods by which that aim is to be pursued is the maintenance and further realisation of human rights and fundamental freedoms; Reaffirming their profound belief in those fundamental freedoms which are the foundation of justice and peace in the world and are best maintained on the one hand by an effective political democracy and on the other by a common understanding and observance of the human rights upon which they depend;

Being resolved, as the governments of European countries which are like-minded and have a common heritage of political traditions, ideals, freedom and the rule of law, to take the first steps for the collective enforcement of certain of the rights stated in the Universal Declaration,

Have agreed as follows—

NOTES

[1]   Headings added according to the provisions of Protocol No 11 (ETS No 155).

Article 1
Obligation to respect human rights

The High Contracting Parties shall secure to everyone within their jurisdiction the rights and freedoms defined in Section 1 of this Convention.

SECTION 1
RIGHTS AND FREEDOMS

Article 2
Right to life

1   Everyone's right to life shall be protected by law. No one shall be deprived of his life intentionally save in the execution of a sentence of a court following his conviction of a crime for which this penalty is provided by law.

2   Deprivation of life shall not be regarded as inflicted in contravention of this article when it results from the use of force which is no more than absolutely necessary—

(a)   in defence of any person from unlawful violence;
(b)   in order to effect a lawful arrest or to prevent the escape of a person lawfully detained;
(c)   in action lawfully taken for the purpose of quelling a riot or insurrection.

Article 3
Prohibition of torture

No one shall be subjected to torture or to inhuman or degrading treatment or punishment.

Article 4
Prohibition of slavery and forced labour

1   No one shall be held in slavery or servitude.

2   No one shall be required to perform forced or compulsory labour.

3   For the purpose of this article the term 'forced or compulsory labour' shall not include—

(a)   any work required to be done in the ordinary course of detention imposed according to the provisions of Article 5 of this Convention or during conditional release from such detention;

(b)   any service of a military character or, in case of conscientious objectors in countries where they are recognised, service exacted instead of compulsory military service;

(c)   any service exacted in case of an emergency or calamity threatening the life or well-being of the community;

(d)   any work or service which forms part of normal civic obligations.

Article 5
Right to liberty and security

1   Everyone has the right to liberty and security of person. No one shall be deprived of his liberty save in the following cases and in accordance with a procedure prescribed by law—

(a)   the lawful detention of a person after conviction by a competent court;

(b)   the lawful arrest or detention of a person for noncompliance with the lawful order of a court or in order to secure the fulfilment of any obligation prescribed by law;

(c)   the lawful arrest or detention of a person effected for the purpose of bringing him before the competent legal authority on reasonable suspicion of having committed an offence or when it is reasonably considered necessary to prevent his committing an offence or fleeing after having done so;

(d)   the detention of a minor by lawful order for the purpose of educational supervision or his lawful detention for the purpose of bringing him before the competent legal authority;

(e)   the lawful detention of persons for the prevention of the spreading of infectious diseases, of persons of unsound mind, alcoholics or drug addicts or vagrants;

(f)   the lawful arrest or detention of a person to prevent his effecting an unauthorised entry into the country or of a person against whom action is being taken with a view to deportation or extradition.

2   Everyone who is arrested shall be informed promptly, in a language which he understands, of the reasons for his arrest and of any charge against him.

3   Everyone arrested or detained in accordance with the provisions of paragraph 1(c) of this article shall be brought promptly before a judge or other officer authorised by law to exercise judicial power and shall be entitled to trial within a reasonable time or to release pending trial. Release may be conditioned by guarantees to appear for trial.

4   Everyone who is deprived of his liberty by arrest or detention shall be entitled to take proceedings by which the lawfulness of his detention shall be decided speedily by a court and his release ordered if the detention is not lawful.

5   Everyone who has been the victim of arrest or detention in contravention of the provisions of this article shall have an enforceable right to compensation.

Article 6
Right to a fair trial

1   In the determination of his civil rights and obligations or of any criminal charge against him, everyone is entitled to a fair and public hearing within a reasonable time by an independent and impartial tribunal established by law. Judgment shall be pronounced publicly but the press and public may be excluded from all or part of the trial in the interests of morals, public order or national security in a democratic society, where the interests of juveniles or the protection of the private life of the parties so require, or to the extent strictly necessary in the opinion of the court in special circumstances where publicity would prejudice the interests of justice.

2   Everyone charged with a criminal offence shall be presumed innocent until proved guilty according to law.

3   Everyone charged with a criminal offence has the following minimum rights—
   (a)   to be informed promptly, in a language which he understands and in detail, of the nature and cause of the accusation against him;
   (b)   to have adequate time and facilities for the preparation of his defence;
   (c)   to defend himself in person or through legal assistance of his own choosing or, if he has not sufficient means to pay for legal assistance, to be given it free when the interests of justice so require;
   (d)   to examine or have examined witnesses against him and to obtain the attendance and examination of witnesses on his behalf under the same conditions as witnesses against him;
   (e)   to have the free assistance of an interpreter if he cannot understand or speak the language used in court.

Article 7
No punishment without law

1   No one shall be held guilty of any criminal offence on account of any act or omission which did not constitute a criminal offence under national or international law at the time when it was committed. Nor shall a heavier penalty be imposed than the one that was applicable at the time the criminal offence was committed.

2   This article shall not prejudice the trial and punishment of any person for any act or omission which, at the time when it was committed, was criminal according to the general principles of law recognised by civilised nations.

Article 8
Right to respect for private and family life

1   Everyone has the right to respect for his private and family life, his home and his correspondence.

2   There shall be no interference by a public authority with the exercise of this right except such as is in accordance with the law and is necessary in a democratic society in the interests of national security, public safety or the economic well-being of the country, for the prevention of disorder or crime, for the protection of health or morals, or for the protection of the rights and freedoms of others.

Article 9
Freedom of thought, conscience and religion

1   Everyone has the right to freedom of thought, conscience and religion; this right includes freedom to change his religion or belief and freedom, either alone or in community with others and in public or private, to manifest his religion or belief, in worship, teaching, practice and observance.

2   Freedom to manifest one's religion or beliefs shall be subject only to such limitations as are prescribed by law and are necessary in a democratic society in the interests of public safety, for the protection of public order, health or morals, or for the protection of the rights and freedoms of others.

Article 10
Freedom of expression

1   Everyone has the right to freedom of expression. This right shall include freedom to hold opinions and to receive and impart information and ideas without interference by public authority and regardless of frontiers. This article shall not prevent States from requiring the licensing of broadcasting, television or cinema enterprises.

2   The exercise of these freedoms, since it carries with it duties and responsibilities, may be subject to such formalities, conditions, restrictions or penalties as are prescribed by law and are necessary in a democratic society, in the interests of national security, territorial integrity or public safety, for the prevention of disorder or crime, for the protection of health or morals, for the protection of the reputation or rights of others, for preventing the disclosure of information received in confidence, or for maintaining the authority and impartiality of the judiciary.

Article 11
Freedom of assembly and association

1   Everyone has the right to freedom of peaceful assembly and to freedom of association with others, including the right to form and to join trade unions for the protection of his interests.

2   No restrictions shall be placed on the exercise of these rights other than such as are prescribed by law and are necessary in a democratic society in the interests of national security or public safety, for the prevention of disorder or crime, for the protection of health or morals or for the protection of the rights and freedoms of others. This article shall not prevent the imposition of lawful restrictions on the exercise of these rights by members of the armed forces, of the police or of the administration of the State.

Article 12
Right to marry

Men and women of marriageable age have the right to marry and to found a family, according to the national laws governing the exercise of this right.

Article 13
Right to an effective remedy

Everyone whose rights and freedoms as set forth in this Convention are violated shall have an effective remedy before a national authority notwithstanding that the violation has been committed by persons acting in an official capacity.

Article 14
Prohibition of discrimination

The enjoyment of the rights and freedoms set forth in this Convention shall be secured without discrimination on any ground such as sex, race, colour, language, religion, political or other opinion, national or social origin, association with a national minority, property, birth or other status.

Article 15
Derogation in time of emergency

1   In time of war or other public emergency threatening the life of the nation any High Contracting Party may take measures derogating from its obligations under this Convention to the extent strictly required by the exigencies of the situation, provided that such measures are not inconsistent with its other obligations under international law.

2   No derogation from Article 2, except in respect of deaths resulting from lawful acts of war, or from Articles 3, 4 (paragraph 1) and 7 shall be made under this provision.

3   Any High Contracting Party availing itself of this right of derogation shall keep the Secretary General of the Council of Europe fully informed of the measures which it has taken and the reasons therefor. It shall also inform the Secretary General of the Council of Europe when such measures have ceased to operate and the provisions of the Convention are again being fully executed.

Article 16
Restrictions on political activity of aliens

Nothing in Articles 10, 11 and 14 shall be regarded as preventing the High Contracting Parties from imposing restrictions on the political activity of aliens.

Article 17
Prohibition of abuse of rights

Nothing in this Convention may be interpreted as implying for any State, group or person any right to engage in any activity or perform any act aimed at the destruction of any of the rights and freedoms set forth herein or at their limitation to a greater extent than is provided for in the Convention.

Article 18
Limitation on use of restrictions on rights

The restrictions permitted under this Convention to the said rights and freedoms shall not be applied for any purpose other than those for which they have been prescribed.

SECTION II
EUROPEAN COURT OF HUMAN RIGHTS

Article 19
Establishment of the Court

To ensure the observance of the engagements undertaken by the High Contracting Parties in the Convention and the Protocols thereto, there shall be set up a European Court of Human Rights, hereinafter referred to as 'the Court'. It shall function on a permanent basis.

Article 20
Number of judges

The Court shall consist of a number of judges equal to that of the High Contracting Parties.

Article 21
Criteria for office

1   The judges shall be of high moral character and must either possess the qualifications required for appointment to high judicial office or be jurisconsults of recognised competence.

2   The judges shall sit on the Court in their individual capacity.

3   During their term of office the judges shall not engage in any activity which is incompatible with their independence, impartiality or with the demands of a full-time office; all questions arising from the application of this paragraph shall be decided by the Court.

Article 22
Election of judges

1   The judges shall be elected by the Parliamentary Assembly with respect to each High Contracting Party by a majority of votes cast from a list of three candidates nominated by the High Contracting Party.

2   The same procedure shall be followed to complete the Court in the event of the accession of new High Contracting Parties and in filling casual vacancies.

Article 23
Terms of office

1   The judges shall be elected for a period of six years. They may be re-elected. However, the terms of office of one-half of the judges elected at the first election shall expire at the end of three years.

2   The judges whose terms of office are to expire at the end of the initial period of three years shall be chosen by lot by the Secretary General of the Council of Europe immediately after their election.

3   In order to ensure that, as far as possible, the terms of office of one-half of the judges are renewed every three years, the Parliamentary Assembly may decide, before proceeding to any subsequent election, that the term or terms of office of one or more judges to be elected shall be for a period other than six years but not more than nine and not less than three years.

4   In cases where more than one term of office is involved and where the Parliamentary Assembly applies the preceding paragraph, the allocation of the terms of office shall be effected by a drawing of lots by the Secretary General of the Council of Europe immediately after the election.

5   A judge elected to replace a judge whose term of office has not expired shall hold office for the remainder of his predecessor's term.

6   The terms of office of judges shall expire when they reach the age of 70.

7   The judges shall hold office until replaced. They shall, however, continue to deal with such cases as they already have under consideration.

Article 24
Dismissal

No judge may be dismissed from his office unless the other judges decide unanimously that he has ceased to fulfil the required conditions.

Article 25
Registry and legal secretaries

The Court shall have a registry, the functions and organisation of which shall be laid down in the rules of the Court. The Court shall be assisted by legal secretaries.

Article 26
Plenary Court

The plenary Court shall—

(a) elect its President and one or two Vice-Presidents for a period of three years; they may be re-elected;
(b) set up Chambers, constituted for a fixed period of time;
(c) elect the Presidents of the Chambers of the Court; they may be re-elected;
(d) adopt the rules of the Court, and
(e) elect the Registrar and one or more Deputy Registrars.

Article 27
Committees, Chambers and Grand Chamber

1   To consider cases brought before it, the Court shall sit in committees of three judges, in Chambers of seven judges and in a Grand Chamber of seventeen judges. The Court's Chambers shall set up committees for a fixed period of time.

2   There shall sit as an *ex officio* member of the Chamber and the Grand Chamber the judge elected in respect of the State Party concerned or, if there is none or if he is unable to sit, a person of its choice who shall sit in the capacity of judge.

3   The Grand Chamber shall also include the President of the Court, the Vice-Presidents, the Presidents of the Chambers and other judges chosen in accordance with the rules of the Court. When a case is referred to the Grand Chamber under Article 43, no judge from the Chamber which rendered the judgment shall sit in the Grand Chamber, with the exception of the President of the Chamber and the judge who sat in respect of the State Party concerned.

Article 28
Declarations of inadmissibility by committees

A committee may, by a unanimous vote, declare inadmissible or strike out of its list of cases an application submitted under Article 34 where such a decision can be taken without further examination. The decision shall be final.

Article 29
Decisions by Chambers on admissibility and merits

1   If no decision is taken under Article 28, a Chamber shall decide on the admissibility and merits of individual applications submitted under Article 34.

2   A Chamber shall decide on the admissibility and merits of inter-State applications submitted under Article 33.

3   The decision on admissibility shall be taken separately unless the Court, in exceptional cases, decides otherwise.

Article 30
Relinquishment of jurisdiction to the Grand Chamber

Where a case pending before a Chamber raises a serious question affecting the interpretation of the Convention or the protocols thereto, or where the resolution of a question before the Chamber might have a result inconsistent with a judgment previously delivered by the Court, the Chamber may, at any time before it has rendered its judgment, relinquish jurisdiction in favour of the Grand Chamber, unless one of the parties to the case objects.

Article 31
Powers of the Grand Chamber

The Grand Chamber shall—

(a) determine applications submitted either under Article 33 or Article 34 when a Chamber has relinquished jurisdiction under Article 30 or when the case has been referred to it under Article 43; and

(b) consider requests for advisory opinions submitted under Article 47.

Article 32
Jurisdiction of the Court

1 The jurisdiction of the Court shall extend to all matters concerning the interpretation and application of the Convention and the protocols thereto which are referred to it as provided in Articles 33, 34 and 47.

2 In the event of dispute as to whether the Court has jurisdiction, the Court shall decide.

Article 33
Inter-State cases

Any High Contracting Party may refer to the Court any alleged breach of the provisions of the Convention and the protocols thereto by another High Contracting Party.

Article 34
Individual applications

The Court may receive applications from any person, non-governmental organisation or group of individuals claiming to be the victim of a violation by one of the High Contracting Parties of the rights set forth in the Convention or the protocols thereto. The High Contracting Parties undertake not to hinder in any way the effective exercise of this right.

Article 35
Admissibility criteria

1 The Court may only deal with the matter after all domestic remedies have been exhausted, according to the generally recognised rules of international law, and within a period of six months from the date on which the final decision was taken.

2 The Court shall not deal with any application submitted under Article 34 that—

(a) is anonymous; or

(b) is substantially the same as a matter that has already been examined by the Court or has already been submitted to another procedure of international investigation or settlement and contains no relevant new information.

3 The Court shall declare inadmissible any individual application submitted under Article 34 which it considers incompatible with the provisions of the Convention or the protocols thereto, manifestly ill-founded, or an abuse of the right of application.

4 The Court shall reject any application which it considers inadmissible under this Article. It may do so at any stage of the proceedings.

Article 36
Third party intervention

1 In all cases before a Chamber of the Grand Chamber, a High Contracting Party one of whose nationals is an applicant shall have the right to submit written comments and to take part in hearings.

2   The President of the Court may, in the interest of the proper administration of justice, invite any High Contracting Party which is not a party to the proceedings or any person concerned who is not the applicant to submit written comments or take part in hearings.

Article 37
Striking out applications

1   The Court may at any stage of the proceedings decide to strike an application out of its list of cases where the circumstances lead to the conclusion that—

(a)   the applicant does not intend to pursue his application; or
(b)   the matter has been resolved; or
(c)   for any other reason established by the Court, it is no longer justified to continue the examination of the application.

However, the Court shall continue the examination of the application if respect for human rights as defined in the Convention and the protocols thereto so requires.

2   The Court may decide to restore an application to its list of cases if it considers that the circumstances justify such a course.

Article 38
Examination of the case and friendly settlement proceedings

1   If the Court declares the application admissible, it shall—

(a)   pursue the examination of the case, together with the representatives of the parties, and if need be, undertake an investigation, for the effective conduct of which the States concerned shall furnish all necessary facilities;

(b)   place itself at the disposal of the parties concerned with a view to securing a friendly settlement of the matter on the basis of respect for human rights as defined in the Convention and the protocols thereto.

2   Proceedings conducted under paragraph 1(b) shall be confidential.

Article 39
Finding of a friendly settlement

If a friendly settlement is effected, the Court shall strike the case out of its list by means of a decision which shall be confined to a brief statement of the facts and of the solution reached.

Article 40
Public hearings and access to documents

1   Hearings shall be in public unless the Court in exceptional circumstances decides otherwise.

2   Documents deposited with the Registrar shall be accessible to the public unless the President of the Court decides otherwise.

Article 41
Just satisfaction

If the Court finds that there has been a violation of the Convention or the protocols thereto, and if the internal law of the High Contracting Party concerned allows only partial reparation to be made, the Court shall, if necessary, afford just satisfaction to the injured party.

Article 42
Judgments of Chambers

Judgments of Chambers shall become final in accordance with the provisions of Article 44, paragraph 2.

Article 43
Referral to the Grand Chamber

1   Within a period of three months from the date of the judgment of the Chamber, any party to the case may, in exceptional cases, request that the case be referred to the Grand Chamber.

2   A panel of five judges of the Grand Chamber shall accept the request if the case raises a serious question affecting the interpretation or application of the Convention or the protocols thereto, or a serious issue of general importance.

3   If the panel accepts the request, the Grand Chamber shall decide the case by means of a judgment.

Article 44
Final judgments

1   The judgment of the Grand Chamber shall be final.

2   The judgment of a Chamber shall become final—
   (a)   when the parties declare that they will not request that the case be referred to the Grand Chamber; or
   (b)   three months after the date of the judgment, if reference of the case to the Grand Chamber has not been requested; or
   (c)   when the panel of the Grand Chamber rejects the request to refer under Article 43.

3   The final judgment shall be published.

Article 45
Reasons for judgments and decisions

1   Reasons shall be given for judgments as well as for decisions declaring applications admissible or inadmissible.

2   If a judgment does not represent, in whole or in part, the unanimous opinion of the judges, any judge shall be entitled to deliver a separate opinion.

Article 46
Binding force and execution of judgments

1   The High Contracting Parties undertake to abide by the final judgment of the Court in any case to which they are parties.

2   The final judgment of the Court shall be transmitted to the Committee of Ministers, which shall supervise its execution.

Article 47
Advisory opinions

1   The Court may, at the request of the Committee of Ministers, give advisory opinions on legal questions concerning the interpretation of the Convention and the protocols thereto.

2   Such opinions shall not deal with any question relating to the content or scope of the rights or freedoms defined in Section 1 of the Convention and the

protocols thereto, or with any other question which the Court or the Committee of Ministers might have to consider in consequence of any such proceedings as could be instituted in accordance with the Convention.

3   Decisions of the Committee of Ministers to request an advisory opinion of the Court shall require a majority vote of the representatives entitled to sit on the Committee.

Article 48
Advisory jurisdiction of the Court

The Court shall decide whether a request for an advisory opinion submitted by the Committee of Ministers is within its competence as defined in Article 47.

Article 49
Reasons for advisory opinions

1   Reasons shall be given for advisory opinions of the Court.

2   If the advisory opinion does not represent, in whole or in part, the unanimous opinion of the judges, any judge shall be entitled to deliver a separate opinion.

3   Advisory opinions of the Court shall be communicated to the Committee of Ministers.

Article 50
Expenditure on the Court

The expenditure on the Court shall be borne by the Council of Europe.

Article 51
Privileges and immunities of judges

The judges shall be entitled, during the exercise of their functions, to the privileges and immunities provided for in Article 40 of the Statute of the Council of Europe and in the agreements made thereunder.

SECTION III[1,2]
MISCELLANEOUS PROVISIONS

NOTES
[1]   Headings in this section added according to the provisions of Protocol No 11 (ETS No 155).
[2]   The articles of this section are renumbered according to the provisions of Protocol No 11 (ETS No 155).

Article 52
Inquiries by the Secretary General

On receipt of a request from the Secretary General of the Council of Europe any High Contracting Party shall furnish an explanation of the manner in which its internal law ensures the effective implementation of any of the provisions of the Convention.

Article 53
Safeguard for existing human rights

Nothing in this Convention shall be construed as limiting or derogating from any of the human rights and fundamental freedoms which may be ensured under the laws of any High Contracting Party or under any other agreement to which it is a Party.

Article 54
Powers of the Committee of Ministers

Nothing in this Convention shall prejudice the powers conferred on the Committee of Ministers by the Statute of the Council of Europe.

Article 55
Exclusion of other means of dispute settlement

The High Contracting Parties agree that, except by special agreement, they will not avail themselves of treaties, conventions or declarations. in force between them for the purpose of submitting, by way of petition, a dispute arising out of the interpretation or application of this Convention to a means of settlement other than those provided for in this Convention.

Article 56
Territorial application

1[2]   Any State may at the time of its ratification or at any time thereafter declare by notification addressed to the Secretary General of the Council of Europe that the present Convention shall, subject to paragraph 4 of this Article, extend to all or any of the territories for whose international relations it is responsible.

2   The Convention shall extend to the territory or territories named in the notification as from the thirtieth day after the receipt of this notification by the Secretary General of the Council of Europe.

3   The provisions of this Convention shall be applied in such territories with due regard, however, to local requirements.

4[2]   Any State which has made a declaration in accordance with paragraph 1 of this article may at any time thereafter declare on behalf of one or more of the territories to which the declaration relates that it accepts the competence of the Court to receive applications from individuals, non-governmental organisations or groups of individuals as provided by Article 34 of the Convention.

NOTES
[1]   Heading added according to the provisions of Protocol No 11 (ETS No 155).
[2]   Text amended according to the provisions of Protocol No 11 (ETS No 155).

Article 57
Reservations

1   Any State may, when signing this Convention or when depositing its instrument of ratification, make a reservation in respect of any particular provision of the Convention to the extent that any law then in force in its territory is not in conformity with the provision. Reservations of a general character shall not be permitted under this article.

2   Any reservation made under this article shall contain a brief statement of the law concerned.

Article 58
Denunciation

1   A High Contracting Party may denounce the present Convention only after the expiry of five years from the date on which it became a party to it and after six months' notice contained in a notification addressed to the Secretary General of the Council of Europe, who shall inform the other High Contracting Parties.

2   Such a denunciation shall not have the effect of releasing the High Contracting Party concerned from its obligations under this Convention in respect of any act which, being capable of constituting a violation of such obligations, may have been performed by it before the date at which the denunciation became effective.

3   Any High Contracting Party which shall cease to be a member of the Council of Europe shall cease to be a Party to this Convention under the same conditions.

4[2]   The Convention may be denounced in accordance with the provisions of the preceding paragraphs in respect of any territory to which it has been declared to extend under the terms of Article 56.

NOTES
[1]   Heading added according to the provisions of Protocol No 11 (ETS No 155).
[2]   Text amended according to the provisions of Protocol No 11 (ETS No 155).

Article 59
Signature and ratification

1   This Convention shall be open to the signature of the members of the Council of Europe. It shall be ratified. Ratifications shall be deposited with the Secretary General of the Council of Europe.

2   The present Convention shall come into force after the deposit of ten instruments of ratification.

3   As regards any signatory ratifying subsequently, the Convention shall come into force at the date of the deposit of its instrument of ratification.

4   The Secretary General of the Council of Europe shall notify all the members of the Council of Europe of the entry into force of the Convention, the names of the High Contracting Parties who have ratified it, and the deposit of all instruments of ratification which may be effected subsequently.

Done at Rome this 4th day of November 1950, in English and French, both texts being equally authentic, in a single copy which shall remain deposited in the archives of the Council of Europe. The Secretary General shall transmit certified copies to each of the signatories.

Protocol [No 1] to the Convention for the Protection of Human Rights and Fundamental Freedoms[1]

Paris, 20.III.1952

The governments signatory hereto, being members of the Council of Europe,

Being resolved to take steps to ensure the collective enforcement of certain rights and freedoms other than those already included in Section 1 of the Convention for the Protection of Human Rights and Fundamental Freedoms signed at Rome on 4 November 1950 (hereinafter referred to as 'the Convention'),

Have agreed as follows—

Article 1
Protection of property

Every natural or legal person is entitled to the peaceful enjoyment of his possessions. No one shall be deprived of his possessions except in the public interest and subject to the conditions provided for by law and by the general principles of international law.

The preceding provisions shall not, however, in any way impair the right of a State to enforce such laws as it deems necessary to control the use of property in accordance with the general interest or to secure the payment of taxes or other contributions or penalties.

NOTES
1   Headings of articles added and text amended according to the provisions of Protocol No 11 (ETS No 155) as from its entry into force.

Article 2
Right to education

No person shall be denied the right to education. In the exercise of any functions which it assumes in relation to education and to teaching, the State shall respect the right of parents to ensure such education and teaching in conformity with their own religious and philosophical convictions.

Article 3
Right to free elections

The High Contracting Parties undertake to hold free elections at reasonable intervals by secret ballot, under conditions which will ensure the free expression of the opinion of the people in the choice of the legislature.

Article 4
Territorial application

Any High Contracting Party may at the time of signature or ratification or at any time thereafter communicate to the Secretary General of the Council of Europe a declaration stating the extent to which it undertakes that the provisions of the present Protocol shall apply to such of the territories for the international relations of which it is responsible as are named therein.

Any High Contracting Party which has communicated a declaration in virtue of the preceding paragraph may from time to time communicate a further declaration modifying the terms of any former declaration or terminating the application of the provisions of this Protocol in respect of any territory.

A declaration made in accordance with this article shall be deemed to have been made in accordance with paragraph 1 of Article 56 of the Convention.

NOTES
1   Text amended according to the provisions of Protocol No 11 (ETS No 155).

Article 5
Relationship to the Convention

As between the High Contracting Parties the provisions of Articles 1, 2, 3 and 4 of this Protocol shall be regarded as additional articles to the Convention and all the provisions of the Convention shall apply accordingly.

Article 6
Signature and ratification

This Protocol shall be open for signature by the members of the Council of Europe, who are the signatories of the Convention; it shall be ratified at the same time as or after the ratification of the Convention. It shall enter into force after the deposit of ten instruments of ratification. As regards any signatory ratifying subsequently, the Protocol shall enter into force at the date of the deposit of its instrument of ratification.

The instruments of ratification shall be deposited with the Secretary General of the Council of Europe, who will notify all members of the names of those who have ratified.

Done at Paris on the 20th day of March 1952, in English and French, both texts being equally authentic, in a single copy which shall remain deposited in the archives of the Council of Europe. The Secretary General shall transmit certified copies to each of the signatory governments.

Protocol No 4 to the Convention for the Protection of Human Rights and Fundamental Freedoms securing certain rights and freedoms other than those already included in the Convention and in the First Protocol thereto[1]

Strasbourg, 16.IX.1963

NOTES
[1] Headings of articles added and text amended according to the provisions of Protocol No 11 (ETS No 155) as from its entry into force.

The governments signatory hereto, being members of the Council of Europe,

Being resolved to take steps to ensure the collective enforcement of certain rights and freedoms other than those already included in Section 1 of the Convention for the Protection of Human Rights and Fundamental Freedoms signed at Rome on 4th November 1950 (hereinafter referred to as the 'Convention') and in Articles 1 to 3 of the First Protocol to the Convention, signed at Paris on 20th March 1952,

Have agreed as follows—

Article 1
Prohibition of imprisonment for debt

No one shall be deprived of his liberty merely on the ground of inability to fulfil a contractual obligation.

Article 2
Freedom of movement

1   Everyone lawfully within the territory of a State shall, within that territory, have the right to liberty of movement and freedom to choose his residence.

2   Everyone shall be free to leave any country, including his own.

3   No restrictions shall be placed on the exercise of these rights other than such as are in accordance with law and are necessary in a democratic society in the interests of national security or public safety, for the maintenance of ordre public, for the prevention of crime, for the protection of health or morals, or for the protection of the rights and freedoms of others.

4   The rights set forth in paragraph 1 may also be subject, in particular areas, to restrictions imposed in accordance with law and justified by the public interest in a democratic society.

Article 3
Prohibition of expulsion of nationals

1   No one shall be expelled, by means either of an individual or of a collective measure, from the territory of the State of which he is a national.

2   No one shall be deprived of the right to enter the territory of the state of which he is a national.

Article 4
Prohibition of collective expulsion of aliens

Collective expulsion of aliens is prohibited.

Article 5
Territorial application

1   Any High Contracting Party may, at the time of signature or ratification of this Protocol, or at any time thereafter, communicate to the Secretary General of the Council of Europe a declaration stating the extent to which it undertakes that the provisions of this Protocol shall apply to such of the territories for the international relations of which it is responsible as are named therein.

2   Any High Contracting Party which has communicated a declaration in virtue of the preceding paragraph may, from time to time, communicate a further declaration modifying the terms of any former declaration or terminating the application of the provisions of this Protocol in respect of any territory.

3[1]   A declaration made in accordance with this article shall be deemed to have been made in accordance with paragraph 1 of Article 56 of the Convention.

4   The territory of any State to which this Protocol applies by virtue of ratification or acceptance by that State, and each territory to which this Protocol is applied by virtue of a declaration by that State under this article, shall be treated as separate territories for the purpose of the references in Articles 2 and 3 to the territory of a State.

5[2]   Any State which has made a declaration in accordance with paragraph 1 or 2 of this Article may at any time thereafter declare on behalf of one or more of the territories to which the declaration relates that it accepts the competence of the Court to receive applications from individuals, non-governmental organisations or groups of individuals as provided in Article 34 of the Convention in respect of all or any of Articles 1 to 4 of this Protocol.

NOTES
[1]   Text amended according to the provisions of Protocol No 11 (ETS No 155).
[2]   Text added according to the provisions of Protocol No 11 (ETS No 155).

Article 6
Relationship to the Convention

As between the High Contracting Parties the provisions of Articles 1 to 5 of this Protocol shall be regarded as additional Articles to the Convention, and all the provisions of the Convention shall apply accordingly.

NOTES
[1] Text amended according to the provisions of Protocol No 11 (ETS No 155).

Article 7
Signature and ratification

1   This Protocol shall be open for signature by the members of the Council of Europe who are the signatories of the Convention; it shall be ratified at the same time as or after the ratification of the Convention. It shall enter into force after the deposit of five instruments of ratification. As regards any signatory ratifying subsequently, the Protocol shall enter into force at the date of the deposit of its instrument of ratification.

2   The instruments of ratification shall be deposited with the Secretary General of the Council of Europe, who will notify all members of the names of those who have ratified.

In witness whereof the undersigned, being duly authorised thereto, have signed this Protocol.

Done at Strasbourg, this 16th day of September 1963, in English and in French, both texts being equally authoritative, in a single copy which shall remain deposited in the archives of the Council of Europe. The Secretary General shall transmit certified copies to each of the signatory states.

Protocol No 6 to the Convention for the Protection of Human Rights and Fundamental Freedoms concerning the Abolition of the Death Penalty[1]

Strasbourg, 28.IV.1983

The member States of the Council of Europe, signatory to this Protocol to the Convention for the Protection of Human Rights and Fundamental Freedoms, signed at Rome on 4 November 1950 (hereinafter referred to as 'the Convention'),

Considering that the evolution that has occurred in several member States of the Council of Europe expresses a general tendency in favour of abolition of the death penalty;

Have agreed as follows—

NOTES
[1] Headings of articles added and text amended according to the provisions of Protocol No 11 (ETS No 155) as from its entry into force.

Article 1
Abolition of the death penalty

The death penalty shall be abolished. No-one shall be condemned to such penalty or executed.

Article 2
Death penalty in time of war

A State may make provision in its law for the death penalty in respect of acts committed in time of war or of imminent threat of war; such penalty shall be applied only in the instances laid down in the law and in accordance with its provisions. The State shall communicate to the Secretary General of the Council of Europe the relevant provisions of that law.

Article 3
Prohibition of derogations

No derogation from the provisions of this Protocol shall be made under Article 15 of the Convention.

Article 4[1]
Prohibition of reservations

No reservation may be made under Article 57 of the Convention in respect of the provisions of this Protocol.

NOTES
[1]   Text amended according to the provisions of Protocol No 11 (ETS No 155).

Article 5
Territorial application

1   Any State may at the time of signature or when depositing its instrument of ratification, acceptance or approval, specify the territory or territories to which this Protocol shall apply.

2   Any State may at any later date, by a declaration addressed to the Secretary General of the Council of Europe, extend the application of this Protocol to any other territory specified in the declaration. In respect of such territory the Protocol shall enter into force on the first day of the month following the date of receipt of such declaration by the Secretary General.

3   Any declaration made under the two preceding paragraphs may, in respect of any territory specified in such declaration, be withdrawn by a notification addressed to the Secretary General. The withdrawal shall become effective on the first day of the month following the date of receipt of such notification by the Secretary General.

Article 6
Relationship to the Convention

As between the States Parties the provisions of Articles 1 and 5 of this Protocol shall be regarded as additional articles to the Convention and all the provisions of the Convention shall apply accordingly.

Article 7
Signature and ratification

The Protocol shall be open for signature by the member States of the Council of Europe, signatories to the Convention. It shall be subject to ratification, acceptance or approval. A member State of the Council of Europe may not ratify, accept or approve this Protocol unless it has, simultaneously or previously, ratified the Convention. Instruments of ratification, acceptance or approval shall be deposited with the Secretary General of the Council of Europe.

Article 8
Entry into force

1   This Protocol shall enter into force on the first day of the month following the date on which five member States of the Council of Europe have expressed their consent to be bound by the Protocol in accordance with the provisions of Article 7.

2   In respect of any member State which subsequently expresses its consent to be bound by it, the Protocol shall enter into force on the first day of the month following the date of the deposit of the instrument of ratification, acceptance or approval.

Article 9
Depositary functions

The Secretary General of the Council of Europe shall notify the member States of the Council of—

(a)   any signature;

(b)   the deposit of any instrument of ratification, acceptance or approval;

(c)   any date of entry into force of this Protocol in accordance with Articles 5 and 8;

(d)   any other act, notification or communication relating to this Protocol.

In witness whereof the undersigned, being duly authorised thereto, have signed this Protocol.

Done at Strasbourg, this 28th day of April 1983, in English and in French, both texts being equally authentic, in a single copy which shall be deposited in the archives of the Council of Europe. The Secretary General of the Council of Europe shall transmit certified copies to each member State of the Council of Europe.

Protocol No 7 to the Convention for the Protection of Human Rights and Fundamental Freedoms[1]

Strasbourg, 22.XI.1984

NOTES
[1]   Headings of articles added and text amended according to the provisions of Protocol No 11 (ETS No 155) as from its entry into force.

The member States of the Council of Europe signatory hereto,

Being resolved to take further steps to ensure the collective enforcement of certain rights and freedoms by means of the Convention for the Protection of Human Rights and Fundamental Freedoms signed at Rome on 4 November 1950 (hereinafter referred to as 'the Convention'),

Have agreed as follows—

Article 1
Procedural safeguards relating to expulsion of aliens

1   An alien lawfully resident in the territory of a State shall not be expelled therefrom except in pursuance of a decision reached in accordance with law and shall be allowed—
      (a)   to submit reasons against his expulsion,
      (b)   to have his case reviewed, and

    (c)   to be represented for these purposes before the competent authority or a person or persons designated by that authority.

2   An alien may be expelled before the exercise of his rights under paragraph 1(a), (b) and (c) of this Article, when such expulsion is necessary in the interests of public order or is grounded on reasons of national security.

Article 2
Right of appeal in criminal matters

1   Everyone convicted of a criminal offence by a tribunal shall have the right to have his conviction or sentence reviewed by a higher tribunal. The exercise of this right, including the grounds on which it may be exercised, shall be governed by law.

2   This right may be subject to exceptions in regard to offences of a minor character, as prescribed by law, or in cases in which the person concerned was tried in the first instance by the highest tribunal or was convicted following an appeal against acquittal.

Article 3
Compensation for wrongful conviction

When a person has by a final decision been convicted of a criminal offence and when subsequently his conviction has been reversed, or he has been pardoned, on the ground that a new or newly discovered fact shows conclusively that there has been a miscarriage of justice, the person who has suffered punishment as a result of such conviction shall be compensated according to the law or the practice of the state concerned, unless it is proved that the nondisclosure of the unknown fact in time is wholly or partly attributable to him.

Article 4
Right not to be tried or punished twice

1   No one shall be liable to be tried or punished again in criminal proceedings under the jurisdiction of the same state for an offence for which he has already been finally acquitted or convicted in accordance with the law and penal procedure of that state.

2   The provisions of the preceding paragraph shall not prevent the reopening of the case in accordance with the law and penal procedure of the State concerned, if there is evidence of new or newly discovered facts, or if there has been a fundamental defect in the previous proceedings, which could affect the outcome of the case.

3   No derogation from this Article shall be made under Article 15 of the Convention.

Article 5
Equality between spouses

Spouses shall enjoy equality of rights and responsibilities of a private law character between them, and in their relations with their children, as to marriage, during marriage and in the event of its dissolution. This Article shall not prevent States from taking such measures as are necessary in the interests of the children.

Article 6
Territorial applications

1   Any State may at the time of signature or when depositing its instrument of ratification, acceptance or approval, specify the territory or territories to which this Protocol shall apply and state the extent to which it undertakes that the provisions of this Protocol shall apply to this or these territories.

2   Any state may at any later date, by a declaration addressed to the Secretary-General of the Council of Europe, extend the application of this Protocol to any other territory specified in the declaration. In respect of such territory the protocol shall enter into force on the first day of the month following the expiration of a period of two months after the date of receipt by the Secretary-General of such declaration.

3   Any declaration made under the two preceding paragraphs may, in respect of any territory specified in such declaration, be withdrawn or modified by a notification addressed to the Secretary-General. The withdrawal or modification shall become effective on the first day of the month following the expiration of a period of two months after the date of receipt of such notification by the Secretary-General.

4[1]   A declaration made in accordance with this Article shall be deemed to have been made in accordance with paragraph 1 of Article 56 of the Convention.

5   The territory of any State to which this Protocol applies by virtue of ratification, acceptance or approval by that State, and each territory to which this Protocol is applied by virtue of a declaration by that State under this Article, may be treated as separate territories for the purpose of the reference in Article 1 to the territory of a State.

6[2]   Any State which has made a declaration in accordance with paragraph 1 or 2 of this Article may at any time thereafter declare on behalf of one or more of the territories to which the declaration relates that it accepts the competence of the Court to receive applications from individuals, non-governmental organisations or groups of individuals as provided in Article 34 of the Convention in respect of Articles 1 to 5 of this Protocol.

NOTES
[1]   Text amended according to the provisions of Protocol No 11 (ETS No 155).
[2]   Text added according to the provisions of Protocol No 11 (ETS No 155).

Article 7[1]
Relationship to the Convention

As between the States Parties, the provisions of Article 1 to 6 of this Protocol shall be regarded as additional Articles to the Convention, and all the provisions of the Convention shall apply accordingly.

NOTES
[1]   Text amended according to the provisions of Protocol No 11 (ETS No 155).

Article 8
Signature and ratification

This Protocol shall be open for signature by member States of the Council of Europe which have signed the Convention. It is subject to ratification, acceptance or approval. A member State of the Council of Europe may not ratify, accept or approve this Protocol without previously or simultaneously ratifying the Convention. Instruments of ratification, acceptance or approval shall be deposited with the Secretary General of the Council of Europe.

Article 9
Entry into force

1   This Protocol shall enter into force on the first day of the month following the expiration of a period of two months after the date on which seven member States of the Council of Europe have expressed their consent to be bound by the Protocol in accordance with the provisions of Article 8.

2   In respect of any member State which subsequently expresses its consent to be bound by it, the Protocol shall enter into force on the first day of the month following the expiration of a period of two months after the date of the deposit of the instrument of ratification, acceptance or approval.

Article 10
Depositary functions

The Secretary General of the Council of Europe shall notify all the member States of the Council of Europe of—

(a)   any signature;

(b)   the deposit of any instrument of ratification, acceptance or approval;

(c)   any date of entry into force of this Protocol in accordance with Articles 6 and 9;

(d)   any other act, notification or declaration relating to this Protocol.

In witness whereof the undersigned, being duly authorised thereto, have signed this Protocol.

Done at Strasbourg this 22nd day of November 1984, in English and French, both texts being equally authentic, in a single copy which shall be deposited in the archives of the Council of Europe. The Secretary General of the Council of Europe shall transmit certified copies to each member State of the Council of Europe.

Appendix 3

European Court of Human Rights
Rules of Court

European Court of Human Rights Rules of Court

(4 November 1998)

The European Court of Human Rights,

Having regard to the Convention for the Protection of Human Rights and Fundamental Freedoms and the Protocols thereto,

Makes the present Rules—

Rule 1
(Definitions)

For the purposes of these Rules unless the context otherwise requires—

(*a*)　the term 'Convention' means the Convention for the Protection of Human Rights and Fundamental Freedoms and the Protocols thereto;

(*b*)　the expression 'plenary Court' means the European Court of Human Rights sitting in plenary session;

(*c*)　the term 'Grand Chamber' means the Grand Chamber of seventeen judges constituted in pursuance of Article 27(1) of the Convention;

(*d*)　the term 'Section' means a Chamber set up by the plenary Court for a fixed period in pursuance of Article 26(*b*) of the Convention and the expression 'President of the Section' means the judge elected by the plenary Court in pursuance of Article 26(*c*) of the Convention as President of such a Section;

(*e*)　the term 'Chamber' means any Chamber of seven judges constituted in pursuance of Article 27(1) of the Convention and the expression 'President of the Chamber' means the judge presiding over such a 'Chamber';

(*f*)　the term 'Committee' means a Committee of three judges set up in pursuance of Article 27(1) of the Convention;

(*g*)　the term 'Court' means either the plenary Court, the Grand Chamber, a Section, a Chamber, a Committee or the panel of five judges referred to in Article 43(2) of the Convention;

(*h*)　the expression *'ad hoc* judge' means any person, other than an elected judge, chosen by a Contracting Party in pursuance of Article 27(2)of the Convention to sit as a member of the Grand Chamber or as a member of a Chamber;

(*i*)　the terms 'judge' and 'judges' mean the judges elected by the Parliamentary Assembly of the Council of Europe or *ad hoc* judges;

(*j*)　the term 'Judge Rapporteur' means a judge appointed to carry out the tasks provided for in Rules 48 and 49;

(*k*)　the term 'Registrar' denotes the Registrar of the Court or the Registrar of a Section according to the context;

(*l*)　the terms 'party' and 'parties' mean
— the applicant or respondent Contracting Parties;
— the applicant (the person, non-governmental organisation or group of individuals) that lodged a complaint under Article 34 of the Convention;

(*m*)　the expression 'third party' means any Contracting State or any person concerned who, as provided for in Article 36(1) and (2) of the Convention, has exercised its right or been invited to submit written comments or take part in a hearing;

(*n*)　the expression 'Committee of Ministers' means the Committee of Ministers of the Council of Europe;

(o)   the terms 'former Court' and 'Commission' mean respectively the European Court and European Commission of Human Rights set up under former Article 19 of the Convention.

TITLE I
ORGANISATION AND WORKING OF THE COURT

CHAPTER I
JUDGES

Rule 2
(Calculation of term of office)

(1)   The duration of the term of office of an elected judge shall be calculated as from the date of election. However, when a judge is re-elected on the expiry of the term of office or is elected to replace a judge whose term of office has expired or is about to expire, the duration of the term of office shall, in either case, be calculated as from the date of such expiry.

(2)   In accordance with Article 23(5) of the Convention, a judge elected to replace a judge whose term of office has not expired shall hold office for the remainder of the predecessor's term.

(3)   In accordance with Article 23(7) of the Convention, an elected judge shall hold office until a successor has taken the oath or made the declaration provided for in Rule 3.

Rule 3
(Oath or solemn declaration)

(1)   Before taking up office, each elected judge shall, at the first sitting of the plenary Court at which the judge is present or, in case of need, before the President of the Court, take the following oath or make the following solemn declaration—

'I swear'—or 'I solemnly declare'—'that I will exercise my functions as a judge honourably, independently and impartially and that I will keep secret all deliberations.'

(2)   This act shall be recorded in minutes.

Rule 4
(Incompatible activities)

In accordance with Article 21(3) of the Convention, the judges shall not during their term of office engage in any political or administrative activity or any professional activity which is incompatible with their independence or impartiality or with the demands of a full-time office. Each judge shall declare to the President of the Court any additional activity. In the event of a disagreement between the President and the judge concerned, any question arising shall be decided by the plenary Court.

Rule 5
(Precedence)

(1)   Elected judges shall take precedence after the President and Vice-Presidents of the Court and the Presidents of the Sections, according to the date of their election; in the event of re-election, even if it is not an immediate re-election, the length of time during which the judge concerned previously held office as a judge shall be taken into account.

(2)   Vice-Presidents of the Court elected to office on the same date shall take precedence according to the length of time they have served as judges. If the length of time they have served as judges is the same, they shall take precedence according to age. The same Rule shall apply to Presidents of Sections.

(3)   Judges who have served the same length of time as judges shall take precedence according to age.

(4)   *Ad hoc* judges shall take precedence after the elected judges according to age.

Rule 6
(Resignation)

Resignation of a judge shall be notified to the President of the Court, who shall transmit it to the Secretary General of the Council of Europe. Subject to the provisions of Rules 24(3) *in fine* and 26(2), resignation shall constitute vacation of office.

Rule 7
(Dismissal from office)

No judge may be dismissed from his or her office unless the other judges, meeting in plenary session, decide by a majority of two-thirds of the elected judges in office that he or she has ceased to fulfil the required conditions. He or she must first be heard by the plenary Court. Any judge may set in motion the procedure for dismissal from office.

CHAPTER II
PRESIDENCY OF THE COURT

Rule 8
(Election of the President and Vice-Presidents of the Court and the Presidents and Vice-Presidents of the Sections)

(1)   The plenary Court shall elect its President, two Vice-Presidents and the Presidents of the Sections for a period of three years, provided that such period shall not exceed the duration of their terms of office as judges. They may be re-elected.

(2)   Each Section shall likewise elect for a renewable period of three years a Vice-President, who shall replace the President of the Section if the latter is unable to carry out his or her duties.

(3)   The Presidents and Vice-Presidents shall continue to hold office until the election of their successors.

(4)   If a President or a Vice-President ceases to be a member of the Court or resigns from office before its normal expiry, the plenary Court or the relevant Section, as the case may be, shall elect a successor for the remainder of the term of that office.

(5)   The elections referred to in this Rule shall be by secret ballot; only the elected judges who are present shall take part. if no judge receives an absolute majority of the elected judges present, a ballot shall take place between the two judges who have received most votes. In the event of a tie, preference shall be given to the judge having precedence in accordance with Rule 5.

Rule 9
(Functions of the President of the Court)

(1)   The President of the Court shall direct the work and administration of the Court. The President shall represent the Court and, in particular, be responsible for its relations with the authorities of the Council of Europe.

(2)   The President shall preside at plenary meetings of the Court, meetings of the Grand Chamber and meetings of the panel of five judges.

(3)   The President shall not take part in the consideration of cases being heard by Chambers except where he or she is the judge elected in respect of a Contracting Party concerned.

Rule 10
(Functions of the Vice-Presidents of the Court)

The Vice-Presidents of the Court shall assist the President of the Court. They shall take the place of the President if the latter is unable to carry out his or her duties or the office of President is vacant, or at the request of the President. They shall also act as Presidents of Sections.

Rule 11
(Replacement of the President and the Vice-Presidents)

If the President and the Vice-Presidents of the Court are at the same time unable to carry out their duties or if their offices are at the same time vacant, the office of President of the Court shall be assumed by a President of a Section or, if none is available, by another elected judge, in accordance with the order of precedence provided for in Rule 5.

Rule 12
(Presidency of Sections and Chambers)

The Presidents of the Sections shall preside at the sittings of the Section and Chambers of which they are members. The Vice-Presidents of the Sections shall take their place if they are unable to carry out their duties or if the office of President of the Section concerned is vacant, or at the request of the President of the Section. Failing that, the judges of the Section and the Chambers shall take their place, in the order of precedence provided for in Rule 5.

Rule 13
(Inability to preside)

Judges of the Court may not preside in cases in which the Contracting Party of which they are nationals or in respect of which they were elected is a party.

Rule 14
(Balanced representation of the sexes)

In relation to the making of appointments governed by this and the following chapter of the present Rules, the Court shall pursue a policy aimed at securing a balanced representation of the sexes.

CHAPTER III
THE REGISTRY

Rule 5
(Election of the Registrar)

(1)   The plenary Court shall elect its Registrar. The candidates shall be of high moral character and must possess the legal, managerial and linguistic knowledge and experience necessary to carry out the functions attaching to the post.

(2)   The Registrar shall be elected for a term of five years and may be re-elected. The Registrar may not be dismissed from office, unless the judges, meeting in plenary

session, decide by a majority of two-thirds of the elected judges in office that the person concerned has ceased to fulfil the required conditions. He or she must first be heard by the plenary Court. Any judge may set in motion the procedure for dismissal from office.

(3)   The elections referred to in this Rule shall be by secret ballot; only the elected judges who are present shall take part. If no candidate receives an absolute majority of the elected judges present, a ballot shall take place between the two candidates who have received most votes. In the event of a tie, preference shall be given, firstly, to the female candidate, if any, and, secondly, to the older candidate.

(4)   Before taking up office, the Registrar shall take the following oath or make the following solemn declaration before the plenary Court or, if need be, before the President of the Court—

'I swear'—or 'I solemnly declare'—'that I will exercise loyally, discreetly and conscientiously the functions conferred upon me as Registrar of the European Court of Human Rights.'

This act shall be recorded in minutes.

Rule 16
(Election of the Deputy Registrars)

(1)   The plenary Court shall also elect two Deputy Registrars on the conditions and in the manner and for the term prescribed in the preceding Rule. The procedure for dismissal from office provided for in respect of the Registrar shall likewise apply. The Court shall first consult the Registrar in both these matters.

(2)   Before taking up office, a Deputy Registrar shall take an oath or make a solemn declaration before the plenary Court or, if need be, before the President of the Court, in terms similar to those prescribed in respect of the Registrar. This act shall be recorded in minutes.

Rule 17
(Functions of the Registrar)

(1)   The Registrar shall assist the Court in the performance of its functions and shall be responsible for the organisation and activities of the Registry under the authority of the President of the Court.

(2)   The Registrar shall have the custody of the archives of the Court and shall be the channel for all communications and notifications made by, or addressed to, the Court in connection with the cases brought or to be brought before it.

(3)   The Registrar shall, subject to the duty of discretion attaching to this office, reply to requests for information concerning the work of the Court, in particular to enquiries from the press.

(4)   General instructions drawn up by the Registrar, and approved by the President of the Court, shall regulate the working of the Registry.

Rule 18
(Organisation of the Registry)

(1)   The Registry shall consist of Section Registries equal to the number of Sections set up by the Court and of the departments necessary to provide the legal and administrative services required by the Court.

(2)   The Section Registrar shall assist the Section in the performance of its functions and may be assisted by a Deputy Section Registrar.

(3)   The officials of the Registry, including the legal secretaries but not the Registrar and the Deputy Registrars, shall be appointed by the Secretary General of the Council of Europe with the agreement of the President of the Court or of the Registrar acting on the President's instructions.

CHAPTER IV
THE WORKING OF THE COURT

Rule 19
(Seat of the Court)

(1)   The seat of the Court shall be at the seat of the Council of Europe at Strasbourg. The Court may, however, if it considers it expedient, perform its functions elsewhere in the territories of the member States of the Council of Europe.

(2)   The Court may decide, at any stage of the examination of an application, that it is necessary that an investigation or any other function be carried out elsewhere by it or one or more of its members.

Rule 20
(Sessions of the plenary Court)

(1)   The plenary sessions of the Court shall be convened by the President of the Court whenever the performance of its functions under the Convention and under these Rules so requires. The President of the Court shall convene a plenary session if at least one-third of the members of the Court so request, and in any event once a year to consider administrative matters.

(2)   The quorum of the plenary Court shall be two-thirds of the elected judges in office.

(3)   If there is no quorum, the President shall adjourn the sitting.

Rule 21
(Other sessions of the Court)

(1)   The Grand Chamber, the Chambers and the Committees shall sit full time. On a proposal by the President, however, the Court shall fix session periods each year.

(2)   Outside those periods the Grand Chamber and the Chambers shall be convened by their Presidents in cases of urgency.

Rule 22
(Deliberations)

(1)   The Court shall deliberate in private. Its deliberations shall remain secret.

(2)   Only the judges shall take part in the deliberations. The Registrar or the designated substitute, as well as such other officials of the Registry and interpreters whose assistance is deemed necessary, shall be present. No other person may be admitted except by special decision of the Court.

(3)   Before a vote is taken on any matter in the Court, the President may request the judges to state their opinions on it.

Rule 23
(Votes)

(1)   The decisions of the Court shall be taken by a majority of the judges present. In the event of a tie, a fresh vote shall be taken and, if there is still a tie, the President shall have a casting vote. This paragraph shall apply unless otherwise provided for in these Rules.

(2)   The decisions and judgments of the Grand Chamber and the Chambers shall be adopted by a majority of the sitting judges. Abstentions shall not be allowed in final votes on the admissibility and merits of cases.

(3)   As a general rule, votes shall be taken by a show of hands. The President may take a roll-call vote, in reverse order of precedence.

(4)   Any matter that is to be voted upon shall be formulated in precise terms.

CHAPTER V
THE CHAMBERS

Rule 24
(Composition of the Grand Chamber)

(1)   The Grand Chamber shall be composed of seventeen judges and three substitute judges.

(2)   The Grand Chamber shall be constituted for three years with effect from the election of the presidential office-holders referred to in Rule 8.

(3)   The Grand Chamber shall include the President and Vice-Presidents of the Court and the Presidents of the Sections. In order to complete the Grand Chamber, the plenary Court shall, on a proposal by its President, divide all the other judges into two groups which shall alternate every nine months and whose membership shall be geographically as balanced as possible and reflect the different legal systems among the Contracting Parties. The judges and substitute judges who are to hear each case referred to the Grand Chamber during each nine-month period shall be designated in rotation within each group; they shall remain members of the Grand Chamber until the proceedings have been completed, even after their terms of office as judges have expired.

(4)   If he or she does not sit as a member of the Grand Chamber by virtue of paragraph 3 of the present Rule, the judge elected in respect of any Contracting Party concerned shall sit as an *ex officio* member of the Grand Chamber in accordance with Article 27(2) and (3) of the Convention.

(5)   (a)   Where any President of a Section is unable to sit as a member of the Grand Chamber, he or she shall be replaced by the Vice-President of the Section.

      (b)   If other judges are prevented from sitting, they shall be replaced by the substitute judges in the order in which the latter were selected under paragraph 3 of the present Rule.

      (c)   If there are not enough substitute judges in the group concerned to complete the Grand Chamber, the substitute judges lacking shall be designated by a drawing of lots amongst the members of the other group.

(6)   (a)   The panel of five judges of the Grand Chamber called upon to consider requests submitted under Article 43 of the Convention shall be composed of
—   the President of the Court,
—   the Presidents or, if they are prevented from sitting, the Vice-Presidents of the Sections other than the Section from which was constituted the Chamber that dealt with the case whose referral to the Grand Chamber is being sought,
—   one further judge designated in rotation from among the judges other than those who dealt with the case in the Chamber.

(*b*)   No judge elected in respect of, or who is a national of, a Contracting Party concerned may be a member of the panel.

(*c*)   Any member of the panel unable to sit shall be replaced by another judge who did not deal with the case in the Chamber, who shall be designated in rotation.

Rule 25
(Setting up of Sections)

(1)   The Chambers provided for in Article 26(*b*) of the Convention (referred to in these Rules as 'Sections') shall be set up by the plenary Court, on a proposal by its President, for a period of three years with effect from the election of the presidential office-holders of the Court under Rule 8. There shall be at least four Sections.

(2)   Each judge shall be a member of a Section. The composition of the Sections shall be geographically and gender balanced and shall reflect the different legal systems among the Contracting Parties.

(3)   Where a judge ceases to be a member of the Court before the expiry of the period for which the Section has been constituted, the judge's place in the Section shall be taken by his or her successor as a member of the Court.

(4)   The President of the Court may exceptionally make modifications to the composition of the Sections if circumstances so require.

(5)   On a proposal by the President, the plenary Court may constitute an additional Section.

Rule 26
(Constitution of Chambers)

(1)   The Chambers of seven judges provided for in Article 27(1) of the Convention for the consideration of cases brought before the Court shall be constituted from the Sections as follows.

(*a*)   The Chamber shall in each case include the President of the Section and the judge elected in respect of any Contracting Party concerned. If the latter judge is not a member of the Section to which the application has been assigned under Rule 51 or 52, he or she shall sit as an *ex officio* member of the Chamber in accordance with Article 27(2) of the Convention. Rule 29 shall apply if that judge is unable to sit or withdraws.

(*b*)   The other members of the Chamber shall be designated by the President of the Section in rotation from among the members of the relevant Section.

(*c*)   The members of the Section who are not so designated shall sit in the case as substitute judges.

(2)   Even after the end of their terms of office judges shall continue to deal with cases in which they have participated in the consideration of the merits.

Rule 27
(Committees)

(1)   Committees composed of three judges belonging to the same Section shall be set up under Article 27(1) of the Convention. After consulting the Presidents of the Sections, the President of the Court shall decide on the number of Committees to be set up.

(2)   The Committees shall be constituted for a period of twelve months by rotation among the members of each Section, excepting the President of the Section.

(3)   The judges of the Section who are not members of a Committee may be called upon to take the place of members who are unable to sit.

(4)   Each Committee shall be chaired by the member having precedence in the Section.

Rule 28
(Inability to sit, withdrawal or exemption)

(1)   Any judge who is prevented from taking part in sittings shall, as soon as possible, give notice to the President of the Chamber.

(2)   A judge may not take part in the consideration of any case in which he or she has a personal interest or has previously acted either as the Agent, advocate or adviser of a party or of a person having an interest in the case, or as a member of a tribunal or commission of inquiry, or in any other capacity.

(3)   If a judge withdraws for one of the said reasons, or for some special reason, he or she shall inform the President of the Chamber, who shall exempt the judge from sitting.

(4)   If the President of the Chamber considers that a reason exists for a judge to withdraw, he or she shall consult with the judge concerned; in the event of disagreement, the Chamber shall decide.

Rule 29
(Ad hoc judges)

(1)   If the judge elected in respect of a Contracting Party concerned is unable to sit in the Chamber or withdraws, the President of the Chamber shall invite that Party to indicate within thirty days whether it wishes to appoint to sit as judge either another elected judge or, as an *ad hoc* judge, any other person possessing the qualifications required by Article 21(1) of the Convention and, if so, to state at the same time the name of the person appointed. The same rule shall apply if the person so appointed is unable to sit or withdraws.

(2)   The Contracting Party concerned shall be presumed to have waived its right of appointment if it does not reply within thirty days.

(3)   An *ad hoc* judge shall, at the opening of the first sitting fixed for the consideration of the case after the judge has been appointed, take the oath or make the solemn declaration provided for in Rule 3. This act shall be recorded in minutes.

Rule 30
(Common interest)

(1)   If several applicant or respondent Contracting Parties have a common interest, the President of the Court may invite them to agree to appoint a single elected judge or *ad hoc* judge in accordance with Article 27(2) of the Convention. If the Parties are unable to agree, the President shall choose by lot, from among the persons proposed as judges by these Parties, the judge called upon to sit *ex officio.*

(2)   In the event of a dispute as to the existence of a common interest, the plenary Court shall decide.

TITLE II
PROCEDURE

CHAPTER I
GENERAL RULES

Rule 31
(Possibility of particular derogations)

The provisions of this Title shall not prevent the Court from derogating from them for the consideration of a particular case after having consulted the parties where appropriate.

Rule 32
(Practice directions)

The President of the Court may issue practice directions, notably in relation to such matters as appearance at hearings and the filing of pleadings and other documents.

Rule 33
(Public character of proceedings)

(1)   Hearings shall be public unless, in accordance with paragraph 2 of this Rule, the Chamber in exceptional circumstances decides otherwise, either of its own motion or at the request of a party or any other person concerned.

(2)   The press and the public may be excluded from all or part of a hearing in the interest of morals, public order or national security in a democratic society, where the interests of juveniles or the protection of the private life of the parties so require, or to the extent strictly necessary in the opinion of the Chamber in special circumstances where publicity would prejudice the interests of justice.

(3)   Following registration of an application, all documents deposited with the Registry, with the exception of those deposited within the framework of friendly-settlement negotiations as provided for in Rule 62, shall be accessible to the public unless the President of the Chamber, for the reasons set out in paragraph 2 of this Rule, decides otherwise, either of his or her own motion or at the request of a party or any other person concerned.

(4)   Any request for confidentiality made under paragraphs 1 or 3 above must give reasons and specify whether the hearing or the documents, as the case may be, should be inaccessible to the public in whole or in part.

Rule 34
(Use of languages)

(1)   The official languages of the Court shall be English and French.

(2)   Before the decision on the admissibility of an application is taken, all communications with and pleadings by applicants under Article 34 of the Convention or their representatives, if not in one of the Court's official languages, shall be in one of the official languages of the Contracting Parties.

(3)   (*a*)   All communications with and pleadings by such applicants or their representatives in respect of a hearing, or after a case has been declared admissible, shall be in one of the Court's official languages, unless the President of the Chamber authorises the continued use of the official language of a Contracting Party.

(b) If such leave is granted, the Registrar shall make the necessary arrangements for the oral or written translation of the applicant's observations or statements.

(4) (a) All communications with and pleadings by Contracting Parties or third parties shall be in one of the Court's official languages. The President of the Chamber may authorise the use of a non-official language.

(b) If such leave is granted, it shall be the responsibility of the requesting party to provide for and bear the costs of interpreting or translation into English or French of the oral arguments or written statements made.

(5) The President of the Chamber may invite the respondent Contracting Party to provide a translation of its written submissions in the or an official language of that Party in order to facilitate the applicant's understanding of those submissions.

(6) Any witness, expert or other person appearing before the Court may use his or her own language if he or she does not have sufficient knowledge of either of the two official languages. In that event the Registrar shall make the necessary arrangements for interpreting or translation.

Rule 35
(Representation of Contracting Parties)

The Contracting Parties shall be represented by Agents, who may have the assistance of advocates or advisers.

Rule 36
(Representation of applicants)

(1) Persons, non-governmental organisations or groups of individuals may initially present applications under Article 34 of the Convention themselves or through a representative appointed under paragraph 4 of this Rule.

(2) Following notification of the application to the respondent Contracting Party under Rule 54(3)(b), the President of the Chamber may direct that the applicant should be represented in accordance with paragraph 4 of this Rule.

(3) The applicant must be so represented at any hearing decided on by the Chamber or for the purposes of the proceedings following a decision to declare the application admissible, unless the President of the Chamber decides otherwise.

(4) (a) The representative of the applicant shall be an advocate authorised to practise in any of the Contracting Parties and resident in the territory of one of them, or any other person approved by the President of the Chamber.

(b) The President of the Chamber may, where representation would otherwise be obligatory, grant leave to the applicant to present his or her own case, subject, if necessary, to being assisted by an advocate or other approved representative.

(c) In exceptional circumstances and at any stage of the procedure, the President of the Chamber may, where he or she considers that the circumstances or the conduct of the advocate or other person appointed under the preceding sub-paragraphs so warrant, direct that the latter may no longer represent or assist the applicant and that the applicant should seek alternative representation.

(5) The advocate or other approved representative, or the applicant in person if he or she seeks leave to present his or her own case, must have an adequate knowledge of one of the Court's official languages. However, leave to use a non-official language may be given by the President of the Chamber under Rule 34(3).

Rule 37
(Communications, notifications and summonses)

(1)   Communications or notifications addressed to the Agents or advocates of the parties shall be deemed to have been addressed to the parties.

(2)   If, for any communication, notification or summons addressed to persons other than the Agents or advocates of the parties, the Court considers it necessary to have the assistance of the Government of the State on whose territory such communication, notification or summons is to have effect, the President of the Court shall apply directly to that Government in order to obtain the necessary facilities.

(3)   The same rule shall apply when the Court desires to make or arrange for the making of an investigation on the spot in order to establish the facts or to procure evidence or when it orders the appearance of a person who is resident in, or will have to cross, that territory.

Rule 38
(Written pleadings)

(1)   No written observations or other documents may be filed after the time-limit set by the President of the Chamber or the Judge Rapporteur, as the case may be, in accordance with these Rules. No written observations or other documents filed outside that time-limit or contrary to any practice direction issued under Rule 32 shall be included in the case file unless the President of the Chamber decides otherwise.

(2)   For the purposes of observing the time-limit referred to in paragraph 1, the material date is the certified date of dispatch of the document or, if there is none, the actual date of receipt at the Registry.

Rule 39
(Interim measures)

(1)   The Chamber or, where appropriate, its President may, at the request of a party or of any other person concerned, or of its own motion, indicate to the parties any interim measure which it considers should be adopted in the interests of the parties or of the proper conduct of the proceedings before it.

(2)   Notice of these measures shall be given to the Committee of Ministers.

(3)   The Chamber may request information from the parties on any matter connected with the implementation of any interim measure it has indicated.

Rule 40
(Urgent notification of an application)

In any case of urgency the Registrar, with the authorisation of the President of the Chamber, may, without prejudice to the taking of any other procedural steps and by any available means, inform a Contracting Party concerned in an application of the introduction of the application and of a summary of its objects.

Rule 41
(Case priority)

The Chamber shall deal with applications in the order in which they become ready for examination. It may, however, decide to give priority to a particular application.

Rule 42
(Measures for taking evidence)

(1)   The Chamber may, at the request of a party or a third party, or of its own motion, obtain any evidence which it considers capable of providing clarification of the facts of the case. The Chamber may, *inter alia,* request the parties to produce documentary evidence and decide to hear as a witness or expert or in any other capacity any person whose evidence or statements seem likely to assist it in the carrying out of its tasks.

(2)   The Chamber may, at any time during the proceedings, depute one or more of its members or of the other judges of the Court to conduct an inquiry, carry out an investigation on the spot or take evidence in some other manner. It may appoint independent external experts to assist such a delegation.

(3)   The Chamber may ask any person or institution of its choice to obtain information, express an opinion or make a report on any specific point.

(4)   The parties shall assist the Chamber, or its delegation, in implementing any measures for taking evidence.

(5)   Where a report has been drawn up or some other measure taken in accordance with the preceding paragraphs at the request of an applicant or respondent Contracting Party, the costs entailed shall be borne by that Party unless the Chamber decides otherwise. In other cases the Chamber shall decide whether such costs are to be borne by the Council of Europe or awarded against the applicant or third party at whose request the report was drawn up or the other measure was taken. In all cases the costs shall be taxed by the President of the Chamber.

Rule 43
(Joinder and simultaneous examination of applications)

(1)   The Chamber may, either at the request of the parties or of its own motion, order the joinder of two or more applications.

(2)   The President of the Chamber may, after consulting the parties, order that the proceedings in applications assigned to the same Chamber be conducted simultaneously, without prejudice to the decision of the Chamber on the joinder of the applications.

Rule 44
(Striking out and restoration to the list)

(1)   When an applicant Contracting Party notifies the Registrar of its intention not to proceed with the case, the Chamber may strike the application out of the Court's list under Article 37 of the Convention if the other Contracting Party or Parties concerned in the case agree to such discontinuance.

(2)   The decision to strike out an application which has been declared admissible shall be given in the form of a judgment. The President of the Chamber shall forward that judgment, once it has become final, to the Committee of Ministers in order to allow the latter to supervise, in accordance with Article 46(2) of the Convention, the execution of any undertakings which may have been attached to the discontinuance, friendly settlement or solution of the matter.

(3)   When an application has been struck out, the costs shall be at the discretion of the Court. If an award of costs is made in a decision striking out an application which has not been declared admissible, the President of the Chamber shall forward the decision to the Committee of Ministers.

(4)   The Court may restore an application to its list if it concludes that exceptional circumstances justify such a course.

CHAPTER II
INSTITUTION OF PROCEEDINGS

Rule 45
(Signatures)

(1)   Any application made under Articles 33 or 34 of the Convention shall be submitted in writing and shall be signed by the applicant or by the applicant's representative.

(2)   Where an application is made by a non-governmental organisation or by a group of individuals, it shall be signed by those persons competent to represent that organisation or group. The Chamber or Committee concerned shall determine any question as to whether the persons who have signed an application are competent to do so.

(3)   Where applicants are represented in accordance with Rule 36, a power of attorney or written authority to act shall be supplied by their representative or representatives.

Rule 46
(Contents of an inter-State application)

Any Contracting Party or Parties intending to bring a case before the Court under Article 33 of the Convention shall file with the registry an application setting out

(*a*)   the name of the Contracting Party against which the application is made;

(*b*)   a statement of the facts;

(*c*)   a statement of the alleged violation(s) of the Convention and the relevant arguments;

(*d*)   a statement on compliance with the admissibility criteria (exhaustion of domestic remedies and the six-month rule) laid down in Article 35(1) of the Convention;

(*e*)   the object of the application and a general indication of any claims for just satisfaction made under Article 41 of the Convention on behalf of the alleged injured party or parties; and

(*f*)   the name and address of the person(s) appointed as Agent;

and accompanied by

(*g*)   copies of any relevant documents and in particular the decisions, whether judicial or not, relating to the object of the application.

Rule 47
(Contents of an individual application)

(1)   Any application under Article 34 of the Convention shall be made on the application form provided by the registry, unless the President of the Section concerned decides otherwise. It shall set out

(*a*)   the name, date of birth, nationality, sex, occupation and address of the applicant;

(*b*)   the name, occupation and address of the representative, if any;

(*c*)   the name of the Contracting Party or Parties against which the application is made;

(*d*)   a succinct statement of the facts;

(*e*)   a succinct statement of the alleged violation(s) of the Convention and the relevant arguments;

(*f*)   a succinct statement on the applicant's compliance with the admissibility criteria (exhaustion of domestic remedies and the six-month rule) laid down in Article 35(1) of the Convention; and (*g*)   the object of the application as well as a general indication of any claims for just satisfaction which the applicant may wish to make under Article 41 of the Convention;

and be accompanied by

    (*h*)   copies of any relevant documents and in particular the decisions, whether judicial or not, relating to the object of the application.

(2)   Applicants shall furthermore

    (*a*)   provide information, notably the documents and decisions referred to in paragraph I (h) above, enabling it to be shown that the admissibility criteria (exhaustion of domestic remedies and the six-month rule) laid down in Article 35(1) of the Convention have been satisfied; and

    (*b*)   indicate whether they have submitted their complaints to any other procedure of international investigation or settlement.

(3)   Applicants who do not wish their identity to be disclosed to the public shall so indicate and shall submit a statement of the reasons justifying such a departure from the normal rule of public access to information in proceedings before the Court. The President of the Chamber may authorise anonymity in exceptional and duly justified cases.

(4)   Failure to comply with the requirements set out in paragraphs 1 and 2 above may result in the application not being registered and examined by the Court.

(5)   The date of introduction of the application shall as a general rule be considered to be the date of the first communication from the applicant setting out, even summarily, the object of the application. The Court may for good cause nevertheless decide that a different date shall be considered to be the date of introduction.

(6)   Applicants shall keep the Court informed of any change of address and of all circumstances relevant to the application.

CHAPTER III
JUDGE RAPPORTEURS

Rule 48
(Inter-State applications)

(1)   Where an application is made under Article 33 of the Convention, the Chamber constituted to consider the case shall designate one or more of its judges as Judge Rapporteur(s), who shall submit a report on admissibility when the written observations of the Contracting Parties concerned have been received. Rule 49(4) shall, in so far as appropriate, be applicable to this report.

(2)   After an application made under Article 33 of the Convention has been declared admissible, the Judge Rapporteur(s) shall submit such reports, drafts and other documents as may assist the Chamber in the carrying out of its functions.

Rule 49
(Individual applications)

(1)   Where an application is made under Article 34 of the Convention, the President of the Section to which the case has been assigned shall designate a judge as Judge Rapporteur, who shall examine the application.

(2)   In their examination of applications Judge Rapporteurs

    (*a*)   may request the parties to submit, within a specified time, any factual information, documents or other material which they consider to be relevant;

    (*b*)   shall, subject to the President of the Section directing that the case be considered by a Chamber, decide whether the application is to be considered by a Committee or by a Chamber.

(3)   Where a case is considered by a Committee in accordance with Article 28 of the Convention, the report of the Judge Rapporteur shall contain

    (*a*)   a brief statement of the relevant facts;

    (*b*)   a brief statement of the reasons underlying the proposal to declare the application inadmissible or to strike it out of the list.

(4)   Where a case is considered by a Chamber pursuant to Article 29(1) of the Convention, the report of the Judge Rapporteur shall contain

    (*a*)   a statement of the relevant facts, including any information obtained under paragraph 2 of this Rule;

    (*b*)   an indication of the issues arising under the Convention in the application;

    (*c*)   a proposal on admissibility and on any other action to be taken, together, if need be, with a provisional opinion on the merits.

(5)   After an application made under Article 34 of the Convention has been declared admissible, the Judge Rapporteur shall submit such reports, drafts and other documents as may assist the Chamber in the carrying out of its functions.

Rule 50
(Grand Chamber proceedings)

Where a case has been submitted to the Grand Chamber either under Article 30 or under Article 43 of the Convention, the President of the Grand Chamber shall designate as Judge Rapporteur(s) one or, in the case of an inter-State application, one or more of its members.

CHAPTER IV
PROCEEDINGS ON ADMISSIBILITY

Inter-State applications
Rule 51

(1)   When an application is made under Article 33 of the Convention, the President of the Court shall immediately give notice of the application to the respondent Contracting Party and shall assign the application to one of the Sections.

(2)   In accordance with Rule 26(1)(*a*), the judges elected in respect of the applicant and respondent Contracting Parties shall sit as *ex officio* members of the Chamber constituted to consider the case. Rule 30 shall apply if the application has been brought by several Contracting Parties or if applications with the same object brought by several Contracting Parties are being examined jointly under Rule 43(2).

(3)   On assignment of the case to a Section, the President of the Section shall constitute the Chamber in accordance with Rule 26(1) and shall invite the respondent Contracting Party to submit its observations in writing on the admissibility of the application. The observations so obtained shall be communicated by the Registrar to the applicant Contracting Party, which may submit written observations in reply.

(4)   Before ruling on the admissibility of the application, the Chamber may decide to invite the parties to submit further observations in writing.

(5)   A hearing on the admissibility shall be held if one or more of the Contracting Parties concerned so requests or if the Chamber so decides of its own motion.

(6)   After consulting the Parties, the President of the Chamber shall fix the written and, where appropriate, oral procedure and for that purpose shall lay down the time-limit within which any written observations are to be filed.

(7)   In its deliberations the Chamber shall take into consideration the report submitted by the Judge Rapporteur(s) under Rule 48(1).

Individual applications

Rule 52
(Assignment of applications to the Sections)

(1)   Any application made under Article 34 of the Convention shall be assigned to a Section by the President of the Court, who in so doing shall endeavour to ensure a fair distribution of cases between the Sections.

(2)   The Chamber of seven judges provided for in Article 27(1) of the Convention shall be constituted by the President of the Section concerned in accordance with Rule 26(1) once it has been decided that the application is to be considered by a Chamber.

(3)   Pending the constitution of a Chamber in accordance with the preceding paragraph, the President of the Section shall exercise any powers conferred on the President of the Chamber by these Rules.

Rule 53
(Procedure before a Committee)

(1)   In its deliberations the Committee shall take into consideration the report submitted by the Judge Rapporteur under Rule 49(3).

(2)   The Judge Rapporteur, if he or she is not a member of the Committee, may be invited to attend the deliberations of the Committee.

(3)   In accordance with Article 28 of the Convention, the Committee may, by a unanimous vote, declare inadmissible or strike out of the Court's list of cases an application where such a decision can be taken without further examination. This decision shall be final.

(4)   If no decision pursuant to paragraph 3 of the present Rule is taken, the application shall be forwarded to the Chamber constituted under Rule 52(2) to examine the case.

Rule 54
(Procedure before a Chamber)

(1)   In its deliberations the Chamber shall take into consideration the report submitted by the Judge Rapporteur under Rule 49(4).

(2)   The Chamber may at once declare the application inadmissible or strike it out of the Court's list of cases.

(3)   Alternatively, the Chamber may decide to
  (*a*)   request the parties to submit any factual information, documents or other material which it considers to be relevant;
  (*b*)   give notice of the application to the respondent Contracting Party and invite that Party to submit written observations on the application;
  (*c*)   invite the parties to submit further observations in writing.

(4)   Before taking its decision on admissibility, the Chamber may decide, either at the request of the parties or of its own motion, to hold a hearing. In that event, unless the Chamber shall exceptionally decide otherwise, the parties shall be invited also to address the issues arising in relation to the merits of the application.

(5)   The President of the Chamber shall fix the procedure, including time–limits, in relation to any decisions taken by the Chamber under paragraphs 3 and 4 of this Rule.

Inter-State and individual applications

Rule 55
(Pleas of inadmissibility)

Any plea of inadmissibility must, in so far as its character and the circumstances permit, be raised by the respondent Contracting Party in its written or oral observations on the admissibility of the application submitted as provided in Rule 51 or 54, as the case may be.

Rule 56
(Decision of a Chamber)

(1)   The decision of the Chamber shall state whether it was taken unanimously or by a majority and shall be accompanied or followed by reasons.

(2)   The decision of the Chamber shall be communicated by the Registrar to the applicant and to the Contracting Party or Parties concerned.

Rule 57
(Language of the decision)

(1)   Unless the Court decides that a decision shall be given in both official languages, all decisions shall be given either in English or in French. Decisions given shall be accessible to the public.

(2)   Publication of such decisions in the official reports of the Court, as provided for in Rule 78, shall be in both official languages of the Court.

CHAPTER V
PROCEEDINGS AFTER THE ADMISSION OF AN APPLICATION

Rule 58
(Inter-State applications)

(1)   Once the Chamber has decided to admit an application made under Article 33 of the Convention, the President of the Chamber shall, after consulting the Contracting Parties concerned, lay down the time-limits for the filing of written observations on the merits and for the production of any further evidence. The President may however, with the agreement of the Contracting Parties concerned, direct that a written procedure is to be dispensed with.

(2)   A hearing on the merits shall be held if one or more of the Contracting Parties concerned so requests or if the Chamber so decides of its own motion. The President of the Chamber shall fix the oral procedure.

(3)   In its deliberations the Chamber shall take into consideration any reports, drafts and other documents submitted by the Judge Rapporteur(s) under Rule 48(2).

Rule 59
(Individual applications)

(1)   Once the Chamber has decided to admit an application made under Article 34 of the Convention, it may invite the parties to submit further evidence and written observations.

(2) A hearing on the merits shall be held if the Chamber so decides of its own motion or, provided that no hearing also addressing the merits has been held at the admissibility stage under Rule 54(4), if one of the parties so requests. However, the Chamber may exceptionally decide that the discharging of its functions under Article 38(1)(*a*) of the Convention does not require a hearing to be held.

(3) The President of the Chamber shall, where appropriate, fix the written and oral procedure.

(4) In its deliberations the Chamber shall take into consideration any reports, drafts and other documents submitted by the Judge Rapporteur under Rule 49(5).

Rule 60
(Claims for just satisfaction)

(1) Any claim which the applicant Contracting Party or the applicant may wish to make for just satisfaction under Article 41 of the Convention shall, unless the President of the Chamber directs otherwise, be set out in the written observations on the merits or, if no such written observations are filed, in a special document filed no later than two months after the decision declaring the application admissible.

(2) Itemised particulars of all claims made, together with the relevant supporting documents or vouchers, shall be submitted, failing which the Chamber may reject the claim in whole or in part.

(3) The Chamber may, at any time during the proceedings, invite any party to submit comments on the claim for just satisfaction.

Rule 61
(Third-party intervention)

(1) The decision declaring an application admissible shall be notified by the Registrar to any Contracting Party one of whose nationals is an applicant in the case, as well as to the respondent Contracting Party under Rule 56(2).

(2) Where a Contracting Party seeks to exercise its right to submit written comments or to take part in an oral hearing, pursuant to Article 36(1) of the Convention, the President of the Chamber shall fix the procedure to be followed.

(3) In accordance with Article 36(2) of the Convention, the President of the Chamber may, in the interests of the proper administration of justice, invite or grant leave to any Contracting State which is not a party to the proceedings, or any person concerned who is not the applicant, to submit written comments or, in exceptional cases, to take part in an oral hearing. Requests for leave for this purpose must be duly reasoned and submitted in one of the official languages, within a reasonable time after the fixing of the written procedure.

(4) Any invitation or grant of leave referred to in paragraph 3 of this Rule shall be subject to any conditions, including time-limits, set by the President of the Chamber. Where such conditions are not complied with, the President may decide not to include the comments in the case file.

(5) Written comments submitted in accordance with this Rule shall be submitted in one of the official languages, save where leave to use another language has been granted under Rule 34(4). They shall be transmitted by the Registrar to the parties to the case, who shall be entitled, subject to any conditions, including time-limits, set by the President of the Chamber, to file written observations in reply.

Rule 62
(Friendly settlement)

(1)   Since an application has been declared admissible, the Registrar, acting on the instructions of the Chamber or its President, shall enter into contact with the parties with a view to securing a friendly settlement of the matter in accordance with Article 38(1)(*b*) of the Convention. The Chamber shall take any steps that appear appropriate to facilitate such a settlement.

(2)   In accordance with Article 38(2) of the Convention, the friendly settlement negotiations shall be confidential and without prejudice to the parties' arguments in the contentious proceedings. No written or oral communication and no offer or concession made in the framework of the attempt to secure a friendly settlement may be referred to or relied on in the contentious proceedings.

(3)   If the Chamber is informed by the Registrar that the parties have agreed to a friendly settlement, it shall, after verifying that the settlement has been reached on the basis of respect for human rights as defined in the Convention and the protocols thereto, strike the case out of the Court's list in accordance with Rule 44(2).

CHAPTER VI
HEARINGS

Rule 63
(Conduct of hearings)

(1)   The President of the Chamber shall direct hearings and shall prescribe the order in which Agents and advocates or advisers of the parties shall be called upon to speak.

(2)   Where a fact-finding hearing is being carried out by a delegation of the Chamber under Rule 42, the head of the delegation shall conduct the hearing and the delegation shall exercise any relevant power conferred on the Chamber by the Convention or these Rules.

Rule 64
(Failure to appear at a hearing)

Where, without showing sufficient cause, a party fails to appear, the Chamber may, provided that it is satisfied that such a course is consistent with the proper administration of justice, nonetheless proceed with the hearing.

Rule 65
(Convocation of witnesses, experts and other persons; costs of their appearance)

(1)   Witnesses, experts and other persons whom the Chamber or the President of the Chamber decides to hear shall be summoned by the Registrar.

(2)   The summons shall indicate
      (a)   the case in connection with which it has been issued;
      (*b*)   the object of the inquiry, expert opinion or other measure ordered by the Chamber or the President of the Chamber;
      (*c*)   any provisions for the payment of the sum due to the person summoned.

(3)   If the persons concerned appear at the request or on behalf of an applicant or respondent Contracting Party, the costs of their appearance shall be borne by that Party unless the Chamber decides otherwise. In other cases, the Chamber shall decide whether such costs are to be borne by the Council of Europe or awarded against the applicant or third party at whose request the person summoned appeared. In all cases the costs shall be taxed by the President of the Chamber.

Rule 66
(Oath or solemn declaration by witnesses and experts)

(1)   After the establishment of the identity of the witness and before testifying, every witness shall take the following oath or make the following solemn declaration—

'I swear'—or 'I solemnly declare upon my honour and conscience'—'that I shall speak the truth, the whole truth and nothing but the truth.'

This act shall be recorded in minutes.

(2)   After the establishment of the identity of the expert and before carrying out his or her task, every expert shall take the following oath or make the following solemn declaration—

'I swear'—or 'I solemnly declare'—'that I will discharge my duty as an expert honourably and conscientiously.'

This act shall be recorded in minutes.

(3)   This oath may be taken or this declaration made before the President of the Chamber, or before a judge or any public authority nominated by the President.

Rule 67
(Objection to a witness or expert; hearing of a person for information purposes)

The Chamber shall decide in the event of any dispute arising from an objection to a witness or expert. It may hear for information purposes a person who cannot be heard as a witness.

Rule 68
(Questions put during hearings)

(1)   Any judge may put questions to the Agents, advocates or advisers of the parties, to the applicant, witnesses and experts, and to any other persons appearing before the Chamber.

(2)   The witnesses, experts and other persons referred to in Rule 42(1) may, subject to the control of the President of the Chamber, be examined by the Agents and advocates or advisers of the parties. In the event of an objection as to the relevance of a question put, the President of the Chamber shall decide.

Rule 69
(Failure to appear, refusal to give evidence or false evidence)

If, without good reason, a witness or any other person who has been duly summoned fails to appear or refuses to give evidence, the Registrar shall, on being so required by the President of the Chamber, inform the Contracting Party to whose jurisdiction the witness or other person is subject. The same provisions shall apply if a witness or expert has, in the opinion of the Chamber, violated the oath or solemn declaration provided for in Rule 66.

Rule 70
(Verbatim record of hearings)

(1)   The Registrar shall, if the Chamber so directs, be responsible for the making of a verbatim record of a hearing. The verbatim record shall include
  (a)   the composition of the Chamber at the hearing;
  (b)   a list of those appearing before the Court, that is to say Agents, advocates and advisers of the parties and any third party taking part;
  (c)   the surnames, forenames, description and address of each witness, expert or other person heard;

(*d*)   the text of statements made, questions put and replies given;

(*e*)   the text of any decision delivered during the hearing by the Chamber or the President of the Chamber.

(2)   If all or part of the verbatim record is in a non-official language, the Registrar shall, if the Chamber so directs, arrange for its translation into one of the official languages.

(3)   The representatives of the parties shall receive a copy of the verbatim record in order that they may, subject to the control of the Registrar or the President of the Chamber, make corrections, but in no case may such corrections affect the sense and bearing of what was said. The Registrar shall lay down, in accordance with the instructions of the President of the Chamber, the time-limits granted for this purpose.

(4)   The verbatim record, once so corrected, shall be signed by the President and the Registrar and shall then constitute certified matters of record.

CHAPTER VII
PROCEEDINGS BEFORE THE GRAND CHAMBER

Rule 71
(Applicability of procedural provisions)

Any provisions governing proceedings before the Chambers shall apply, *mutatis mutandis,* to proceedings before the Grand Chamber.

Rule 72
(Relinquishment of jurisdiction by a Chamber in favour of the Grand Chamber)

(1)   In accordance with Article 30 of the Convention, where a case pending before a Chamber raises a serious question affecting the interpretation of the Convention or the protocols thereto or where the resolution of a question before it might have a result inconsistent with a judgment previously delivered by the Court, the Chamber may, at any time before it has rendered its judgment, relinquish jurisdiction in favour of the Grand Chamber, unless one of the parties to the case has objected in accordance with paragraph 2 of this Rule. Reasons need not be given for the decision to relinquish.

(2)   The Registrar shall notify the parties of the Chamber's intention to relinquish jurisdiction. The parties shall have one month from the date of that notification within which to file at the Registry a duly reasoned objection. An objection which does not fulfil these conditions shall be considered invalid by the Chamber.

Rule 73
(Request by a party for referral of a case to the Grand Chamber)

(1)   In accordance with Article 43 of the Convention, any party to a case may exceptionally, within a period of three months from the date of delivery of the judgment of a Chamber, file in writing at the Registry a request that the case be referred to the Grand Chamber. The party shall specify in its request the serious question affecting the interpretation or application of the Convention or the protocols thereto, or the serious issue of general importance, which in its view warrants consideration by the Grand Chamber.

(2)   A panel of five judges of the Grand Chamber constituted in accordance with Rule 24(6) shall examine the request solely on the basis of the existing case file. It shall accept the request only if it considers that the case does raise such a question or issue. Reasons need not be given for a refusal of the request.

(3)   If the panel accepts the request, the Grand Chamber shall decide the case by means of a judgment.

CHAPTER VIII
JUDGMENTS

Rule 74
(Contents of the judgment)

(1)   A judgment as referred to in Articles 42 and 44 of the Convention shall contain—

    (a)   the names of the President and the other judges constituting the Chamber concerned, and the name of the Registrar or the Deputy Registrar;

    (b)   the dates on which it was adopted and delivered;

    (c)   a description of the parties;

    (d)   the names of the Agents, advocates or advisers of the parties;

    (e)   an account of the procedure followed;

    (f)   the facts of the case;

    (g)   a summary of the submissions of the parties;

    (h)   the reasons in point of law;

    (i)   the operative provisions;

    (j)   the decision, if any, in respect of costs;

    (k)   the number of judges constituting the majority;

    (l)   where appropriate, a statement as to which text is authentic.

(2)   Any judge who has taken part in the consideration of the case shall be entitled to annex to the judgment either a separate opinion, concurring with or dissenting from that judgment, or a bare statement of dissent.

Rule 75
(Ruling on just satisfaction)

(1)   Where the Chamber finds that there has been a violation of the Convention, it shall give in the same judgment a ruling on the application of Article 41 of the Convention if that question, after being raised in accordance with Rule 60, is ready for decision; if the question is not ready for decision, the Chamber shall reserve it in whole or in part and shall fix the further procedure.

(2)   For the purposes of ruling on the application of Article 41 of the Convention, the Chamber shall, as far as possible, be composed of those judges who sat to consider the merits of the case. Where it is not possible to constitute the original Chamber, the President of the Court shall complete or compose the Chamber by drawing lots.

(3)   The Chamber may, when affording just satisfaction under Article 41 of the Convention, direct that if settlement is not made within a specified time, interest is to be payable on any sums awarded.

(4)   If the Court is informed that an agreement has been reached between the injured party and the Contracting Party liable, it shall verify the equitable nature of the agreement and, where it finds the agreement to be equitable, strike the case out of the list in accordance with Rule 44(2).

Rule 76
(Language of the judgment)

(1)   Unless the Court decides that a judgment shall be given in both official languages, all judgments shall be given either in English or in French. Judgments given shall be accessible to the public.

(2)   Publication of such judgments in the official reports of the Court, as provided for in Rule 78, shall be in both official languages of the Court.

Rule 77
(Signature, delivery and notification of the judgment)

(1)   Judgments shall be signed by the President of the Chamber and the Registrar.

(2)   The judgment may be read out at a public hearing by the President of the Chamber or by another judge delegated by him or her. The Agents and representatives of the parties shall be informed in due time of the date of the hearing. Otherwise the notification provided for in paragraph 3 of this Rule shall constitute delivery of the judgment.

(3)   The judgment shall be transmitted to the Committee of Ministers. The Registrar shall send certified copies to the parties, to the Secretary General of the Council of Europe, to any third party and to any other person directly concerned. The original copy, duly signed and sealed, shall be placed in the archives of the Court.

Rule 78
(Publication of judgments and other documents)

In accordance with Article 44(3) of the Convention, final judgments of the Court shall be published, under the responsibility of the Registrar, in an appropriate form. The Registrar shall in addition be responsible for the publication of official reports of selected judgments and decisions and of any document which the President of the Court considers it useful to publish.

Rule 79
(Request for interpretation of a judgment)

(1)   A party may request the interpretation of a judgment within a period of one year following the delivery of that judgment.

(2)   The request shall be filed with the Registry. It shall state precisely the point or points in the operative provisions of the judgment on which interpretation is required.

(3)   The original Chamber may decide of its own motion to refuse the request on the ground that there is no reason to warrant considering it. Where it is not possible to constitute the original Chamber, the President of the Court shall complete or compose the Chamber by drawing lots.

(4)   If the Chamber does not refuse the request, the Registrar shall communicate it to the other party or parties and shall invite them to submit any written comments within a time-limit laid down by the President of the Chamber. The President of the Chamber shall also fix the date of the hearing should the Chamber decide to hold one. The Chamber shall decide by means of a judgment.

Rule 80
(Request for revision of a judgment)

(1)   A party may, in the event of the discovery of a fact which might by its nature have a decisive influence and which, when a judgment was delivered, was unknown to the Court and could not reasonably have been known to that party, request the Court, within a period of six months after that party acquired knowledge of the fact, to revise that judgment.

(2)   The request shall mention the judgment of which revision is requested and shall contain the information necessary to show that the conditions laid down in

paragraph 1 have been complied with. It shall be accompanied by a copy of all supporting documents. The request and supporting documents shall be filed with the Registry.

(3)   The original Chamber may decide of its own motion to refuse the request on the ground that there is no reason to warrant considering it. Where it is not possible to constitute the original Chamber, the President of the Court shall complete or compose the Chamber by drawing lots.

(4)   If the Chamber does not refuse the request, the Registrar shall communicate it to the other party or parties and shall invite them to submit any written comments within a time-limit laid down by the President of the Chamber. The President of the Chamber shall also fix the date of the hearing should the Chamber decide to hold one. The Chamber shall decide by means of a judgment.

Rule 81
(Rectification of errors in decisions and judgments)

Without prejudice to the provisions on revision of judgments and on restoration to the list of applications, the Court may, of its own motion or at the request of a party made within one month of the delivery of a decision or a judgment, rectify clerical errors, errors in calculation or obvious mistakes.

CHAPTER IX
ADVISORY OPINIONS

Rule 82

In proceedings relating to advisory opinions the Court shall apply, in addition to the provisions of Articles 47, 48 and 49 of the Convention, the provisions which follow. It shall also apply the other provisions of these Rules to the extent to which it considers this to be appropriate.

Rule 83

The request for an advisory opinion shall be filed with the Registry. It shall state fully and precisely the question on which the opinion of the Court is sought, and also

(a)   the date on which the Committee of Ministers adopted the decision referred to in Article 47(3) of the Convention;

(b)   the names and addresses of the person or persons appointed by the Committee of Ministers to give the Court any explanations which it may require.

The request shall be accompanied by all documents likely to elucidate the question.

Rule 84

(1)   On receipt of a request, the Registrar shall transmit a copy of it to all members of the Court.

(2)   The Registrar shall inform the Contracting Parties that the Court is prepared to receive their written comments.

Rule 85

(1)   The President of the Court shall lay down the time-limits for filing written comments or other documents.

(2)   Written comments or other documents shall be filed with the Registry. The Registrar shall transmit copies of them to all the members of the Court, to the Committee of Ministers and to each of the Contracting Parties.

Rule 86

After the close of the written procedure, the President of the Court shall decide whether the Contracting Parties which have submitted written comments are to be given an opportunity to develop them at an oral hearing held for the purpose.

Rule 87

If the Court considers that the request for an advisory opinion is not within its consultative competence as defined in Article 47 of the Convention, it shall so declare in a reasoned decision.

Rule 88

(1)   Advisory opinions shall be given by a majority vote of the Grand Chamber. They shall mention the number of judges constituting the majority.

(2)   Any judge may, if he or she so desires, attach to the opinion of the Court either a separate opinion, concurring with or dissenting from the advisory opinion, or a bare statement of dissent.

Rule 89

The advisory opinion shall be read out in one of the two official languages by the President of the Court, or by another judge delegated by the President, at a public hearing, prior notice having been given to the Committee of Ministers and to each of the Contracting Parties.

Rule 90

The opinion, or any decision given under Rule 87, shall be signed by the President of the Court and by the Registrar. The original copy, duly signed and sealed, shall be placed in the archives of the Court. The Registrar shall send certified copies to the Committee of Ministers, to the Contracting Parties and to the Secretary General of the Council of Europe.

CHAPTER X
LEGAL AID

Rule 91

(1)   The President of the Chamber may, either at the request of an applicant lodging an application under Article 34 of the Convention or of his or her own motion , grant free legal aid to the applicant in connection with the presentation of the case from the moment when observations in writing on the admissibility of that application are received from the respondent Contracting Party in accordance with Rule 54(3)(*b*), or where the time-limit for their submission has expired.

(2)   Subject to Rule 96, where the applicant has been granted legal aid in connection with the presentation of his or her case before the Chamber, that grant shall continue in force for purposes of his or her representation before the Grand Chamber.

Rule 92

Legal aid shall be granted only where the President of the Chamber is satisfied
- (*a*)   that it is necessary for the proper conduct of the case before the Chamber;
- (*b*)   that the applicant has insufficient means to meet all or part of the costs entailed.

Rule 93

(1) In order to determine whether or not applicants have sufficient means to meet all or part of the costs entailed, they shall be required to complete a form of declaration stating their income, capital assets and any financial commitments in respect of dependants, or any other financial obligations. The declaration shall be certified by the appropriate domestic authority or authorities.

(2) The Contracting Party concerned shall be requested to submit its comments in writing.

(3) After receiving the information mentioned in paragraphs 1 and 2 above, the President of the Chamber shall decide whether or not to grant legal aid. The Registrar shall inform the parties accordingly.

Rule 94

(1) Fees shall be payable to the advocates or other persons appointed in accordance with Rule 36(4). Fees may, where appropriate, be paid to more than one such representative.

(2) Legal aid may be granted to cover not only representatives' fees but also travelling and subsistence expenses and other necessary expenses incurred by the applicant or appointed representative.

Rule 95

On a decision to grant legal aid, the Registrar shall
   (*a*)   fix the rate of fees to be paid in accordance with the legal-aid scales in force;
   (*b*)   the level of expenses to be paid.

Rule 96

The President of the Chamber may, if satisfied that the conditions stated in Rule 92 are no longer fulfilled, revoke or vary a grant of legal aid at any time.

TITLE III
TRANSITIONAL RULES

Rule 97
(Judges' terms of office)

The duration of the terms of office of the judges who were members of the Court at the date of the entry into force of Protocol No 11 to the Convention shall be calculated as from that date.

Rule 98
(Presidency of the Sections)

For a period of three years from the entry into force of Protocol No 11 to the Convention,
   (*a*)   the two Presidents of Sections who are not simultaneously Vice-Presidents of the Court and the Vice-Presidents of the Sections shall be elected for a term of office of eighteen months;
   (*b*)   the Vice-Presidents of the Sections may not be immediately re-elected.

Rule 99
(Relations between the Court and the Commission)

(1)   In cases brought before the Court under Article 5(4) and (5) of Protocol No 11 to the Convention the Court may invite the Commission to delegate one or more of its members to take part in the consideration of the case before the Court.

(2)   In cases referred to in the preceding paragraph the Court shall take into consideration the report of the Commission adopted pursuant to former Article 31 of the Convention.

(3)   Unless the President of the Chamber decides otherwise, the said report shall be made available to the public through the Registrar as soon as possible after the case has been brought before the Court.

(4)   The remainder of the case file of the Commission, including all pleadings, in cases brought before the Court under Article 5(2)–(5) of Protocol No 11 shall remain confidential unless the President of the Chamber decides otherwise.

(5)   In cases where the Commission has taken evidence but has been unable to adopt a report in accordance with former Article 31 of the Convention, the Court shall take into consideration the verbatim records, documentation and opinion of the Commission's delegations arising from such investigations.

Rule 100
(Chamber and Grand Chamber proceedings)

(1)   In cases referred to the Court under Article 5(4) of Protocol No 11 to the Convention, a panel of the Grand Chamber constituted in accordance with Rule 24(6) shall determine, solely on the basis of the existing case file, whether a Chamber or the Grand Chamber is to decide the case.

(2)   If the case is decided by a Chamber, the judgment of the Chamber shall, in accordance with Article 5(4) of Protocol No 11, be final and Rule 73 shall be inapplicable.

(3)   Cases transmitted to the Court under Article 5(5) of Protocol No 11 shall be forwarded by the President of the Court to the Grand Chamber.

(4)   For each case transmitted to the Grand Chamber under Article 5(5) of the Protocol No 11, the Grand Chamber shall be completed by judges designated by rotation within one of the groups mentioned in Rule 24(3), the cases being allocated to the groups on an alternate basis.

Rule 101
(Grant of legal aid)

Subject to Rule 96, in cases brought before the Court under Article 5(2)–(5) of Protocol No 11 to the Convention, a grant of legal aid made to an applicant in the proceedings before the Commission or the former Court shall continue in force for the purposes of his or her representation before the Court.

Rule 102
(Request for interpretation or revision of a judgment)

(1)   Where a party requests interpretation or revision of a judgment delivered by the former Court, the President of the Court shall assign the request to one of the Sections in accordance with the conditions laid down in Rule 51 or 52, as the case may be.

(2)   The President of the relevant Section shall, notwithstanding Rules 79(3) and 80(3), constitute a new Chamber to consider the request.

(3)   The Chamber to be constituted shall include as *ex officio* members
    (*a*)   the President of the Section;

and, whether or not they are members of the relevant Section,
    (*b*)   the judge elected in respect of any Contracting Party concerned or, if he or she is unable to sit, any judge appointed under Rule 29;
    (*c*)   any judge of the Court who was a member of the original Chamber that delivered the judgment in the former Court.

(4)   (*a*)   The other members of the Chamber shall be designated by the President of the Section by means of a drawing of lots from among the members of the relevant Section.

    (*b*)   The members of the Section who are not so designated shall sit in the case as substitute judges.

TITLE IV
FINAL CLAUSES

Rule 103
(Amendment or suspension of a Rule)

(1)   Any Rule may be amended upon a motion made after notice where such a motion is carried at the next session of the plenary Court by a majority of all the members of the Court. Notice of such a motion shall be delivered in writing to the Registrar at least one month before the session at which it is to be discussed. On receipt of such a notice of motion, the Registrar shall inform all members of the Court at the earliest possible moment.

(2)   A Rule relating to the internal working of the Court may be suspended upon a motion made without notice, provided that this decision is taken unanimously by the Chamber concerned. The suspension of a Rule shall in this case be limited in its operation to the particular purpose for which it was sought.

Rule 104
(Entry into force of the Rules)

The present Rules shall enter into force on 1 November 1998.

Index